The Nice Girl's Guide to Good Behaviour

The Nice Girl's Guide to Good Behaviour

by Monica Redlich

Illustrated by Anna K. Zinkeisen

"Per Ardua ad Astra" *

PALAZZO

This edition published in the United Kingdom in 2004 by

Palazzo Editions Limited
15 Gay Street,
Bath, BA1 2PH

Originally published in England in 1935 by Hamish Hamilton, London.

Designed by Bernard Higton

Printed and bound in China

ISBN 0-9545103-2-1

A catalogue record for this book is available from the British Library

* *"Through Struggle to the Stars"*

CONTENTS

Part III. Private Occasions

Part IV. Advanced Instruction

Part V. Cause and Effect

FOREWORD

The nice young girl, setting out from her schoolroom into the great world of ordinary life, is generally given every sort of advice but that which will be of most use to her. She is, it is true, told how to walk, how to dress, how to dance, how to curtsy, how to make up her face – all the serious activities of her own life and those of the people about her. But it is in *abstract* advice that her mentors fail her. She is bluntly told to

Be nice
Be polite
Be bright
Be charming
Be thoughtful

and simply left to get on with it. Thus equipped for life, the poor girl might well be forgiven if she sat down and burst into tears. What use is counsel like this to her? She *wants* to be nice. She *longs* to be polite, be bright, be charming, be thoughtful, and so forth. They represent her highest ideals – but she does not know how to achieve them. *No one has told her*.

It is to fill this appalling gap that the following book has been written. In it, after much research and extensive inquiry, I have collected every occasion for kindness and niceness that the young girl is likely to encounter. Indexed, cross-referenced, and cataloged, they provide, I hope, a complete guide to really outstanding behavior, and the girl who follows them closely will be in a class by herself.

The advice I have given here is, above all things, *practical*. It begins where most others leave off. Instead of saying vaguely, "Be kind," "Be sympathetic," "Be helpful," I have given definite instances for putting these aims into action. They range from kindness to a fellow-guest at a house-party who has fewer evening dresses than you have to sympathy for men of unduly sensitive natures. And for each occasion I have suggested not only what to *think* but – even more important – *what to say about it*. For it is no good having nice thoughts if you do not know how to express them. A word in time can often make all the difference to somebody else's happiness, and thereby, I know, to your own. The girl who knows *what to say* and *when to say it* has the secret of perfect behavior. If she speaks to her friends on the lines set down in this book, her acquaintance will be sought, her sympathy clamored for, her brilliance a byword; and the remarks that people will make about her behind her back would astonish her, if she could hear them.

THE NICE GIRL'S GUIDE

PART I
BEGINNING

I. The Nice Girl and Her Surroundings: What to Know and What to Say

The first problem which faces any sensitive girl is the question of what to feel and – still more – what to *say* about herself, her friends, and her surroundings in general. You want to begin as you mean to go on. Unless you are ready with suitable kind remarks for every occasion, you may easily miss some chance you would always regret.

The essential thing to remember is that facts have several angles. The following, for example, are different aspects of one unvarying truth.

"Jane is marrying Thomas."

"She's hooked him, my dear."

"He knew from the first that he'd have to marry money."

"Well, we all know what *that* means."

"Some people say it's a love-match."

There is *of course* no question of failing to speak the truth. It is simply a question of *considering your hearer*. To present that aspect of a topic which will give most pleasure and happiness is to speak the truth in a far finer manner than by slavishly clinging to so-called accuracy.

FEATURES

A. Your Own

Compliments upon her eyes, skin, etc., never cease to surprise a girl of modest nature. This of course will be obvious in the way you receive them; but it would be wrong and discourteous to be so much surprised that you were not able to answer.

The actual wording of the reply to a compliment is quite immaterial. The following are suggested.

> "Oh, Mr. Blenkinsop."
> "Darling, you are a comic."
> "Oh, do you think so?"

What is far more important is the meaning these words convey. All three mean the same. A nice girl, when she speaks them, implies quite simply:

> "No one has ever commended my eyes before. I should not myself have ventured to think them so pretty, but I have of course unlimited faith in your judgement. Allow me to suggest, however, that their present brilliance may be primarily due to the animation caused by your company."

This formal acknowledgement should go far to prove to your friend that you are exactly the sort of girl he hoped you were.

B. Other People's

The nice girl is far above petty jealousy, and will never try to make out that her friends are not good-looking. You will, I know, be anxious to say all you can in their favour, and will do your best to discount any trifling blemishes. The following remarks combine kindness with absolute honesty.

"Oh, but I think Mary's *charming*. One really hardly notices those teeth."

"Darling Cynthia – so *bright*. You'd never suppose that she's ten years older than I am."

Even should your friend be hopelessly plain, you will want to stand by her. Admit her plainness (for one cannot *lie*), but point out that she has a sweet nature.

If a friend should ask you herself what you think of her features, there are many ways of showing how generously you admire them. For example:

"Everyone says you look charming, when your face is in repose."

"They always say a big nose is a sign of character."

"What nonsense, my dear – you don't look wicked *at all*."

MAKEUP

It has to be remembered that different people hold different views about the question of rouge, lipstick, etc. You, having a perfect complexion, will not mind admitting that you need no makeup whatsoever beyond a little face-powder; but I know that you are broad-minded enough to feel not the slightest intolerance about people who do make up. In fact, you would pretend that you did so yourself, if it seemed likely to put them at their ease.

Men with innocent minds are often deluded by artful makeup, and will think a girl wonderful who is simply *covered* with paint. If someone says to you "Oh, look at that heavenly girl – she's just like a rosebud," it is only honourable to clear up his unfortunate misapprehension.

With old gentlemen, you will have no hesitation in saying with simple candor, "I think rouge is simply *disgusting*." You will of course be careful not to make this remark when your own girl friends are in earshot. It might upset them.

For instance, if you met a woman whose beautiful complexion was palpably due to Art, you could prevent her feeling the slightest envy of your own pure skin by observing courteously "We *all* have perfect complexions nowadays, don't we?"

Similarly, to a woman who is a little older than you you might say, with obvious friendliness, "I dare say I shall make up myself, when I begin to need it."

To girls who are just beginning, you will of course be kind. Do not pretend that they look all right. Say "But, darling, you *can't* go about like that," and show them why, so that they will not repeat their error. Even if you do not find time to do this at the beginning of an evening, but are obliged to do it when the party is at its height, it is better to do it then than to leave her in ignorance.

THE REST OF YOU

Ankles, nice hands, and so on are possessions of which every young girl may be proud. You will have to recognize, however, that men take an interest in other parts of your person, such as, for example, the legs, etc. You must know this, but you must never, never think about it, and you will readily appreciate why I am giving you no remarks upon it. It is all very unfortunate, but it is life.

CLOTHES

A. Your Own

I know very well that the pains you take over your clothes are not due to any thought of *calling attention* to yourself. You simply want to be neat and clean and not bring discredit upon anybody whom you may be going about with. If one of your friends should try to reproach you with what she calls "vanity" and "extravagance," you must explain this to her, making clear, with your unfailing sympathy, that you quite understand she has not the same problems to face. You could say, for example, glancing respectfully at the clothes she has on, "My dear, it must be *heavenly* not to have to bother."

No girl *expects* compliments upon her clothes, any more than she does upon her features (see *Features*). She should however know how to reply to them, for a really nice man (see p. 33) will always take the first opportunity of expressing his admiration for the clothes she is wearing. Indeed, if he does not you may begin to suspect that he is *not nice*, though it does sometimes happen that a man remains silent because he is so much enthralled by the mere fact of your presence that ordinary conversation is entirely beyond him.

The best and most courteous reply to a compliment is "I'm so glad you like it." This, though formal in itself, can by a trifling chance of intonation convey any or all of the following sentiments:

"I *am* so pleased. I chose it entirely for you."

"Well, I'm glad you've had the decency to notice it."

"I am thanking you because it is customary to do so, but I assure you your views on the color of my hat leave me absolutely unmoved."

"How marvelous that you, whom I respect so fervently, should have had the condescension to notice what I was wearing."

"Oh, so you like it, do you?"

The remarks of older people upon your clothes should be largely discounted, for there is no denying that elders are out of date (see p. 83). But if someone should say that your smartest clothes are too old for you, you can pay a graceful tribute to their greater knowledge of life by some such remark as "Oh? Do you think so? Well, I'm sure you ought to know."

For other remarks upon clothes see *Insults* (p. 105).

B. Other People's

It is always nice to make some little comment when you see your friends in new clothes. They are probably feeling apprehensive about their appearance, and a word in season may make all the difference to their peace of mind. You may like to reassure them, for instance, by saying:

"You're so lucky – you look charming in anything."

Or again, if they are not well-to-do, you will want to show them that at least you do not suspect them of extravagance. You might very well say:

"It *is* nice, isn't it, that clothes have come down so much lately."

Should they ask you to guess what they paid for a dress or a hat, it is flattering to their judgment to name the lowest price you can think of.

If you see a great friend ready dressed for some special occasion, and obviously a little too much pleased with her clothes, it is only kind to recall her to a sense of proportion. You might say, very nicely: "What are you going to wear this afternoon?"

If friends who are older than you begin to dress with exaggerated and unsuitable smartness, the least you can do is to bring into the conversation some kindly phrased reminder of their age.

Should you happen to be with a girl friend, watching the clothes at some public gathering, you may easily find some little opportunity of

saying things which you would not otherwise like to. Her new electric-blue satin you have of course tried to praise; but should you see someone in the crowd wearing a similar dress, nothing could be easier, or kinder, than to comment laughingly: "It's extraordinary how *vulgar* blue satin makes some people look." If you are careful to look away from her dress as you say this, she can have *no* grounds for supposing that you mean the remark to be personal.

C. Men's

So many women simply take a man's clothes for granted that you will earn a quite disproportionate amount of gratitude by making some courteous little comment upon them. If, for example, you said to a shy man, "I *love* you in that suit," he might be so much heartened that he would say things which otherwise he would not have the courage to say at all.

The sort of remark I suggest for general purposes would be one of the following:

"That suit certainly makes the most of your figure."

"It looks as if it was *made* for you."

"What beautiful tweed. It looks quite like Harris."

And, if you have been on friendly terms with a man but feel that he is sometimes lacking in refinement of mind, you might say:

"My friend John Brown goes to *such* a good tailor. You must let me give you the name."

YOUR MIND

A. Disposition

I need hardly say anything about this here, for it is bound up with the question of kindness, which is my chief preoccupation (and yours) throughout all this book. It is well to remember, however, that you cannot show *all* your personality to *everyone*. Different people naturally call out different aspects of it; and, while not suggesting for one moment that you should be insincere, I would remind you that it is a very simple kindness to allow them to see those aspects of your mind which are likely to appeal to them most. Thus with an ordinary cultured Englishman you would naturally admit your tremendous affection for dogs; but should you happen to meet a minor poet you would save him from feeling eccentric by entering into his tirade against dog-lovers and frankly confessing that there are times when you hate the brutes yourself.

Similarly, you would never conceal from a young married friend that you simply adore tiny babies, and think hers the most exquisite one that you ever set eyes on. With people of broader outlook, however (young men, confirmed bachelors, and so forth), you could with equal honesty admit that you think babies hideous and their manners unhygienic. But then again, with a man whom your instinct told you you might some day come to regard with something more than esteem (see p. 120), you would be exceptionally careful not to venture a remark like this, which might unintentionally wound him. It is all, as I say, a question of *adaptation*.

B. What You Know

By "what you know" I mean for the moment odd scraps of knowledge which are still left over from school – dates, facts, weights and measures, and other data which is admirable in its way but totally useless for the serious business of life. Here I refer you very earnestly to *An Index to Culture* (p. 70). One word of warning I should give you almost with anguish, if I were not so sure that you are not the person to need it: *Girls who know things are intolerable*.

You can see it for yourself. They are assertive. They think they know best about everything, and attempt to put people right. They upset perfectly normal conversations by dragging in remarks about William of Orange or the Decline of the Roman Empire, and in fact they try to make up for their lack of feminine charm by parading their so-called learning. You, fortunately, are not like this. You know very well that *sweetness* and *sympathy* far outweigh these pathetic displays of pedantry, and I feel quite sure you have done your best to live up to the well-proved maxim that true culture consists in forgetting all that you learned at school.

Even with topics that are not necessarily *school* ones, the same sort of attitude holds good. I have heard of girls who read all the leading articles in their daily paper each morning, simply in order to seem well informed about the principal news of the day. How foolish – indeed, how *selfish*! The nice, the thoughtful, the unselfish girl considers other people. She knows that men have a far better grasp upon public affairs, etc., than she has. She knows they have information to impart, and that they like to impart it (see p. 103).

This does not mean that you have not a thirst for knowledge. Indeed, it means quite the reverse.

The things you want to know about are endless. They include, for example:

Salmon fishing.
India.
Government reconstruction.
Drains.
Wave-lengths.
The Budget.
Homer.
Mr. Roosevelt.
and a hundred other topics besides.

All you ask is that your informant be *nice* (see *How to Know Nice People*, p. 33). When you find yourself next to a man who is able to give you detailed instruction upon them, your pleasure will be so *open* that he will realize at once you are someone quite out of the ordinary.

Although you do not pretend to be clever yourself, you must never let it be thought that you despise girls who *are* clever. You quite realise that some people are good at *one* thing, and some at another; and you do your utmost to praise them and to make their qualifications known.

If a friend of yours who is clever appears to feel her lack of social attraction, do not let her be unhappy. Agree, if you like, that she was not an outstanding success at dear So-and-so's party; but you might well console her by saying "But, darling, you're clever."

Again if she knows something that you do not know (see p. 24), you will not be the slightest bit jealous. You will show your respect by observing "But, then, you're so *clever*."

And, finally, you will whenever possible give public proof of your admiration for her. If, for example, you are making her known to a roomful of your particular friends, you can instantly show them the kind of girl she is if you say as you introduce her "This is Jane – she's *terribly* clever."

YOUR BACKGROUND

Any reference to your home, your education, and your background will of course be guided entirely by your company. What to some people would be boasting would to others seem the grossest understatement, and you will say only that which is certain not to cause offence or ill-feeling. The following series of graded statements should I think make this clear.

Your school.

"Yes, I went to Binksville."
"I was only at Binksville."
"I was at a place called Binksville."

Your car.

"Our funny old bone-shaker."
"Daddy's Daimler."
"The car."

Your relations.

"My unspeakable aunts."
"My darling old aunties."
"My aunt, Lady Tonks."

Your home.

"An enormous old place."

"A little place in the country."

"It's so *close* to *nature*."

"It's deadly dull."

Your family.

"Mother was a de Vere."

"Mother's funny."

"Roland is a horrid little tough."

"Roland's quite a man of the world."

"Roland is a soldier."

"Roland is in the Guards."

Further examples of such graded statements you can easily think out for yourself. Like every other remark you make, they are guided purely by consideration for others. There is no question of insincerity (see p. 13). Once you know what anyone would like to feel about your family (that they are wonderful, important, *parvenu*, nobody, etc.) you will I know find a real satisfaction in adapting your information so as to give him pleasure.

2. Meeting People

As I have said, you are making the most of yourself *not for your own sake but for other people's*. Obviously you cannot be as unselfish as you wish unless you meet people to whom you can really be of use. *You must meet people*. The more you go about, to parties and theaters and dances and all other places where you will be properly appreciated, the more chance you have of achieving that ultimate usefulness which is your most earnest desire.

So go everywhere. One word of warning, though, in case you should think I mean literally go *everywhere*, and accept *every* invitation that comes to you. I do not mean, for instance, go twice a week to tea with old ladies who knew you when you were a baby and think that you are one still. In fact you need never go to tea with old ladies who knew you when you were a baby, for it is idle to hope that, now you are no longer a baby, you can bring the same happiness into their lives. Nor do I mean go to scrambled-egg parties with girls who knew you at school, who have now come up to London to make their fortunes, and who live in bedsitting rooms. You are at an age when your health is of great importance, and nothing less than a five-course dinner in a really good restaurant is sufficient to keep you well. For the same reason, you will of course not go out indiscriminately with young men in subordinate positions, for you realize how uncomfortable they would feel at having to entertain you in cheap places. You must use your discretion. Rather than snatch at every invitation, as some girls might, you will think what is *best* and *wisest* for the person who invites you, and if consideration demands it you will unhesitatingly refuse.

But there are countless occasions when you do not have to deny yourself: when, on the contrary, your duty is to go where you are invited, to meet people, and to be nice to them. These occasions may be classified as *parties*: cocktail parties, theater parties, garden parties, restaurant parties, picnic parties, Ascot parties, swimming parties, and indeed every kind of party where nice people gather together for the purpose of being kind to one another (see p. 73). There, if anywhere, you will meet the sort of people whom it is your ambition to help.

You may think, as many girls do, that the friends whom you used to know at school would be pleasant companions for you just now. Of course this is so, to a large extent: I do not want you *ever* to be disloyal to your old playmates, but you will very soon find that they themselves make difficulties which it is hard for you to get over.

If they are unattractive, they are apt to feel injured because they do not know many nice people. For this, of course, you must pity them; but they go so far as to *want you to introduce them to all your friends*, and this lack of sensibility will stamp them at once as unsuitable associates for you.

If, on the other hand, they are pretty, they will almost certainly be so jealous and uneasy that you cannot have anything to do with them. Knowing very well that they would suffer by the comparison, they will make every attempt to *prevent* you from becoming introduced to the nice friends whom they have got to know.

With the best will in the world, you could not *like* people who have minds like this. You will, of course, continue to be perfectly friendly with these girls whom you were at school with, but you will make it your business not to see them more than you can possibly help.

Two classes of schoolfriends, however, call for a slightly different attitude. If you know a girl who is very rich and entertains a great deal, it is only kind of you to be friends with her. Surrounded as she is by flatterers and spongers, she has no means of knowing who her real friends are, and your regular presence at her parties and entertainments may make all the difference to her.

Schoolfriends with older brothers may also be regarded a little differently. A household like this is the very sort of place that you ought to visit: there are few things more delightful for a young girl like yourself than to be allowed an intimate glimpse of happy English family life.

You will find it extraordinarily easy to begin meeting people. Everyone is anxious to help you. Even your parents, old-fashioned though they may be, realize that your future would look blank indeed if you were not encouraged to begin making friends of your own. You will receive countless invitations, many of which you will be perfectly right to accept. And wherever you go, to parties of every kind, your charm, your kindness, and your perfect manners will make people want to invite you to more parties, and still more parties. In fact you have only to be yourself, and the world will throw open its doors for you.

This does not mean, of course, that you should not keep a watch on your behavior. The really nice girl is *perpetually* careful not to let down her own high standards; and, while not rigidly "conventional" in the strict, old-fashioned sense, you will do nothing that your better nature warns you to be ashamed of.

For instance, there is one way of meeting people that everybody very rightly deplores; and that is the vulgar and objectionable practice popularly known as picking-up. I need hardly even warn you against it, I know. The idea shocks you quite as much as it shocks me. But you must not carry your prejudices too far. True helpfulness may require you at times to override petty convention. Supposing, for instance, that you are sitting alone in a hotel lounge or some similar place, and a man who is obviously nice comes up to you and ventures some gentlemanly remark about the weather. You must obey the promptings of instinct, and regard this as a formal introduction. These are democratic days, and it would never do for you to be haughty and "stand-offish." You might miss untold opportunities.

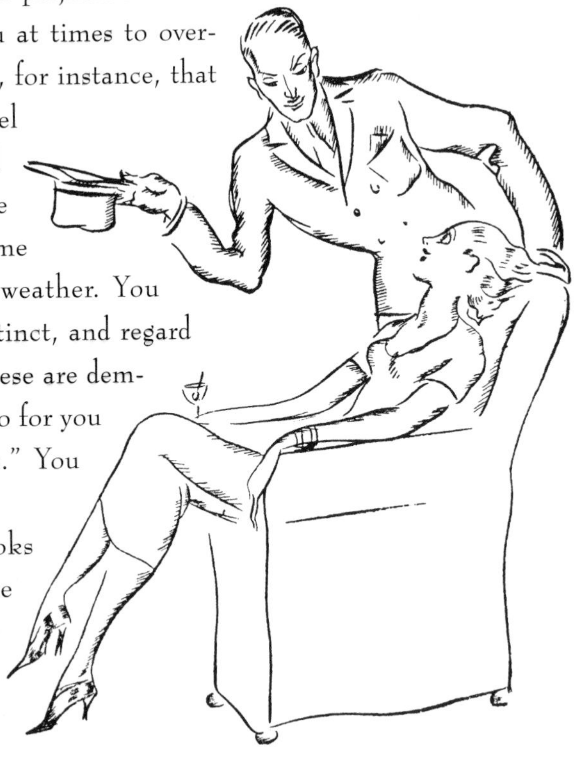

Similarly, if a man who looks lonely has the courtesy to ask if he may sit opposite you in an empty railway-carriage, it is only right to answer with a willing smile.

And if you should happen to drop your glove in a really *good* street, like Piccadilly, and a man whom you have noticed coming along picks it up and returns it to you, your thanks might well form the start of quite a warm friendship.

But, as I say, for the degrading habit of "picking-up" persons of the opposite sex you will have absolutely no toleration.

HOW TO KNOW NICE PEOPLE

It is of the utmost importance to be able to distinguish nice people from those who are not nice. A girl may pay deeply for her own inexperience. Now that you are going about so much, and are meeting new people every day, it is essential that you should begin to discriminate. It is essential to know *which are the nice ones*.

Young girls are often very foolish about this question, and base their ideas of niceness on the most ridiculous things. I have known them like a man because he was musical, or handsome. I have even known them imagine themselves in love because their new friend had blue eyes.

This will not do, and you know very well that it will not. Common sense is essential in friendship as in everything else. Niceness is a question of character, not of looks or of flashy abilities. You want to *understand* character; to learn to look for the little signs which express it, and to base your judgement upon these signs alone. For some men seem nice, but are not so, and unless you know just what to look for you may be sadly deceived.

Is he *steady*? Has he a good job, which carries a reasonable income? You can judge a man by the position he has attained, and you do not want to know anyone who is flighty and thoughtless. If he has not a post himself, what about his father? Heredity counts; and a man whose father has made a success of his work may well be supposed to inherit his parent's steadiness.

Is he well educated? I do not, of course, mean the narrow or "book" kind of learning, but does he understand life in its wider aspects? It is a sure sign of good education if a man knows his way about London: if he knows, not only the restaurants, etc., at which a girl like yourself should be seen, but the tables in each which a thoughtful person would book for you, and the outstanding dishes and wines which each place has to offer. A man like this will, of course, know the plays, cabarets, and similar spectacles which it is advisable to see, and will want you to visit them in order to have the pleasure of discussing them with you.

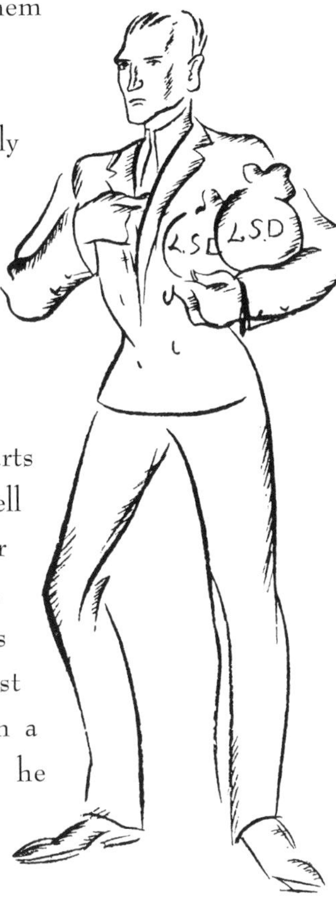

Is he strong-minded? Nothing so perfectly answers this query as a man's behavior with waiters. If he gets what he asks for, and quickly, with the merest lift of his eyebrows and no waste of time saying "Please," you may be sure he has a strength of character which you could never fail to respect.

Is he generous? Long before a man starts giving you presents (see *Presents*), you can tell if he has a generous nature. He will never make you walk while he is looking after you, and if he has not a car he will be punctilious about obtaining taxis. (Men who suggest riding in buses are irrevocably mean.) In a dozen similar ways he will show that he rates your pleasure and comfort above any petty economies.

Has he a serious nature? A friend is no friend unless he has your interests seriously at heart. Would he be always willing to help you? If you were unhappy, or lonely, and needed him to take you somewhere and distract your mind, can you be sure that he would make no excuse of a so-called previous engagement? You do not, of *course*, want to take him away from his other friends: you only want to be certain that he would not fail you at need.

For ordinary friendship, these qualities are absolutely all you require. You are not snobbish or exacting. You ask only for someone you can *trust* and *respect*. It is pleasanter, of course, if a man has innate good taste and expresses it (see *Features* and *Clothes, Your Own*), but a little education can soon teach him this, and friendship with you may do wonders.

Later on, you may come to have somewhat higher ideals (see *Love, True*); but, for the moment, you simply want to get to know as many nice people as possible. The more you know, the wider will be your comprehension and the greater your power of doing good. You will very soon see that good looks and so forth are supremely unimportant. It hardly even matters if a man does not dance. The plainest and least talented men have often the most beautiful characters. Look for a man's good qualities. Test him by the tests which I have suggested above. You will be surprised to find how many superficially unattractive men prove entirely worthy of your friendship.

3. Getting On

Now comes a very important moment. You are going about as you ought to, and have begun getting to know people. You have, in fact, met somebody whom you can instantly classify as really, thoroughly nice. You like him, and he of course likes you. You feel he is the sort of person you could help. *What happens next?*

Naturally, his one ambition is to see you again. Realizing this, you will do what you can for him in an unobtrusive way; but you must remember one infallible rule. *Some men are shy, and some men are not shy*. If your new friend says, "Come on – be a sport" or "By Jove, we must meet again, mustn't we," you will easily know that he is not one of the shy ones. In fact, with such people it is better to be slightly shy yourself. You do not at all costs want to make yourself appear cheap. Accept their invitations for a run down to Henley, or a cinema the following evening, but with less excitement than you actually feel. I have known girls who went so far as to *refuse* such a man's first invitation, staking all on the chance that he will ask them again. I do not myself recommend such unmannerly tactics.

Supposing this self-assured but otherwise charming person should suggest taking you on somewhere after a cocktail party or driving you home from the tennis club. You must not say, "Oh, how lovely," and smile all over your face. Nothing is worse for a man than to encourage his natural vanity. Answer with a certain nonchalance, "Well, that *would* be nice" (this will become much easier after you have practiced it a little), and add that you really are dying for something to eat, or longing for a little fresh air, or anything that will make quite clear to him that the pleasure of his company is the last thing in your mind.

Sometimes even the men who are not shy have not all the opportunities they could wish for. You may, for example, meet one of them when you are positively surrounded with mothers, aunts, and other people who would jealously prevent your talking to him, or with those base-minded people who are given to gossip and scandal (see *Scandal*). In such a case, it is only kind to help him a little. You could engage in a brisk conversation with your neighbor about the delightful little place where you *always* go for lunch when you are alone, mentioning its name several times. She will forget it, but the anxious listener who is talking to your aunt about Gandhi will not fail to keep it in mind.

If all else fails, and conversation remains appallingly general, I suggest that you should lead the discussion round to numbers. Say lightly how stupid some people are at remembering them, and instance your telephone number, which many of your friends forget. A well-bred man would instantly reply with his own telephone number, compare them, prove how easy they were to remember, and pass unobtrusively on to the multiplication table.

It is, however, to the shy men that you must give your most careful attention. Sometimes an otherwise delightful person may carry shyness to such an extent that he will not even realise that he *does* want to see you again. You must, of course, help him. Very likely you are shy yourself, but this is no time to think about your own little troubles. Give him a lead. Say that the country must be lovely just now, and does he often drive out in it. Or that you hear he plays polo and when is he going to ask you to come and watch. Or even that you *are* so tired of this party, and couldn't he take you home.

A shy man like this will naturally continue to be shy even when he is taking you home. Here again it is only kind to help him. Men who are not shy, of course, will not need your assistance; in fact, you may sometimes be glad to find they are driving their own car and not taking you home by taxi, for that means they must have at least one hand on the wheel. But with a shy man it is all very different. It was you who realized that he wanted to see you again. It is you who will realize that he wants to put his arm round you, and perhaps talk to you about the starlight, or perhaps not. By making things easy for him, you will earn his deep if unspoken gratitude, and very possibly more.

I need hardly say that you do not ask him in when you reach your home. To do so on a *first* meeting would be far from suitable (though here again, if you feel either that he is very lonely or that you are yourself, it may be more truly generous to override these petty conventions). However: when the front door shuts behind you, and you stand in the hall listening to the hum of the departing taxi and feeling a delightful tingle on the bridge of your nose[1], you may think to yourself with a quite understandable pride, "Now I have really begun to be helpful to other people."

1. Owing to the darkness of night, the bad state of the roads, and the consequent difficulties of precision, it is here that the tingling will almost certainly be felt.

THE NICE GIRL'S GUIDE

PART II
PUBLIC OCCASIONS

I. A Guide to Public Appearance

It is customary nowadays for young girls to behave in public in a perfectly ladylike manner. This will, I know, be a great relief to you, but you must not think it absolves you from any further effort. Orthodox mannerly behavior in itself is not enough; you want what the poet has so beautifully called "that little extra something some others haven't got."

So in the following pages I have not given you an exhaustive and finicky manual of the proper etiquette for important public occasions. This you have no doubt known from your childhood up, or if not you can easily learn from books of much narrower scope than mine. I have selected only those occasions which afford you some special opportunity.

Ascot – This is a horse-racing event that takes place every June – it is also an outstanding social occasion; it is very popular – and free from the "rougher" element sometimes conspicuous at *The Derby* (see p. 53) An unrivalled chance of studying human nature is provided by the fact that *all nice people have their names on*. The young girl is thus able to check at a glance her own opinion of different people's character. (See *How to Know Nice People*, p. 33).

If her escort wants to back a horse for her, she should stifle any puerile scruples and allow him the pleasure of doing so. A man who is nice will certainly use his own money for the purpose, and she can thus feel that, even if she loses, her conscience is perfectly clear.

Ballet, The – It will show how closely you follow the Art of the Ballet if you say to your escort during the evening, "I'm sure I've heard that tune before, somewhere."

Close observation of the steps of the dancers will certainly prompt you to observe, "Well, I don't see anything wonderful in *that*." And it will prove your quick perception of human character if you remark of the girl who does most of the dancing, "Bony, isn't she? She's just like my second cousin Agatha."

Boat Race, The – The annual rowing contest between Oxford and Cambridge universities is held on the Thames in London, and has become a famous sporting occasion. The race itself is usually over before one has even realized that the boats have passed – which is more than can be said for the Henley Regatta (see p. 54), which lasts for *days*. One of the most unselfish things that a girl can do for a friend is to go with him to the Boat Race. Once there, she can show her passionate interest in the spectacle by remarks such as:

"They *are* rowing fast, aren't they?"

"Which boat is which?"

"It's quite *exciting*, isn't it!"

Charity Events – It is well known that any nice girl will be only too pleased to devote her free time to helping out at fund-raising events such as fêtes and charity performances of plays – it is of course vital that your positioning at these events is such that your services are of most benefit to those around you.

Charity Bazaars – If you are selling at a charity bazaar, it is your principal duty to look as nice and attractive as you can, in order to make everyone want to buy things from you. However much you may want to help with the preparations beforehand, you must remember that two days' hard physical labor are not likely to leave you looking your best, and must leave all these technical details to those whose appearance does not matter.

Try if you possibly can to praise the stalls of your friends. Even if, by the intrigue which always goes on in such places, the stall for which you were ideally suited has been allotted to friends of the organizers, you must rise above petty resentment. You might say, for example: "I'm so glad you've got a really easy stall this time," or "One can always trust Jennifer to make the *most* of herself."

Charity Matinées – When giving your services as a program seller, you will want to do your utmost for the charity which is to benefit: to throw yourself heart and soul into your work. You do not want to take the easy jobs: you would feel almost offended if you were asked to undertake any less exacting post than the stalls. I should make this perfectly clear from the outset; and if people try to urge upon you the delight of selling programs to the gallery, you might say that if *that* is how they feel it would be nice for them to go there themselves.

It is a good plan to count your takings while the play is actually in progress, in order to be able to report upon them punctually. A few objectionable people may tend to protest, but the fact that notes rustle and silver cannot be handled silently is not your fault. When the various totals are compared and you find that yours is the highest, you must be kind to the people who have done much less well than you have, and congratulate them upon their efforts. For you know (whatever jealous remarks are made) that your success has nothing to do with having sold in the stalls. An attractive appearance and an unselfish nature meet with reward in spite of themselves, and you feel nothing but charity for the girls who have not your advantages.

Cinemas – You must remember that at the cinema, as elsewhere, you have other people to think of besides yourself. The friend who has taken you calls for your consideration; and, as long as he does not *materially* interrupt your concentration upon the film, you will, I feel sure, consider him.

Commemoration Balls (See also *Dances*) – Each year, many of the Oxford and Cambridge university colleges hold summer Commemoration Balls, to celebrate their founding. I hope you will derive real pleasure from these dignified functions, and appreciate to the full the poetic quality of university moonlight. But do please remember that undergraduates are very young, and exist only on allowances from their parents. It would be far from kind of you to take their mind from the present, and allow them to entertain any lasting notions of impossible romance. They should at the moment have practically *no* thoughts outside their books.

Concerts – If you let someone take you to a concert, you will want him to be quite sure that you are enjoying yourself. It is only polite to murmur some words of appreciation ("Beautiful!" "Exquisite!" – "Pretty" is hardly strong enough) as soon as you gather that a piece is really over; but do not be misled by the deceptive pauses during which nobody claps. If while everyone else is applauding you sit quite silent with your hands tightly clasped together, you will give your escort the great pleasure of knowing you are so much moved that you have entirely forgotten your surroundings.

Court, Presentation at – If you are selected to be a débutante (see also p. 51), the most important highlight of the season will be your presentation to the Monarch, which symbolically marks your entrance into the adult world. I do not need to say that good behaviour is imperative at this momentous occasion. The precise etiquette of presentation at Their Majesties' Courts does not come within my province. I will, however,

remind you that should some pushing person in the ante-room take the chair (and thus the precedence) that you well know should have been yours, you must bear this rudeness with fortitude and make no remark. If it happens, though, during her maneuvers, that your heel comes down sharply upon the top of her foot, thus causing her considerable pain, this is obviously no fault of yours, and you need not apologize as you once more occupy your rightful position.

Cricket – Cricket is the most English of all games; one could hardly imagine an English summer without its Saturday cricket. Apart from the Eton and Harrow match (see *Lord's*), cricket occurs mainly in the country. It is played almost exclusively by boys and men – girls do not in general care to get within range of a cricket ball. Should you find yourself in a house party where no alternative amusement is offered, you will, of course, be delighted to spend a whole afternoon doing absolutely nothing but look at cricket. You will, I know, want to show an intelligent interest in the game, and the following questions should provoke a maximum of interest in the people around you.

"Which side is batting?"
"Why did he drop it?"
"How much longer is it till tea-time?"

Dances – Dances are of so many kinds that I have listed the most important of them under separate heads (see *Commemoration Balls*, *Débutantes' Dances*, *Hunt Balls*, *Regimental Dances*; see also *Parties*). I need hardly say that your behavior at all of them will be that of a nice, quiet young English girl: but I am here going to mention a very simple rule which should influence *all* your behavior, on any occasion whatever.

What do you look like? What is your type of beauty? Do not be surprised at this question here. You dress according to your looks, I know: but do you *behave* to suit them? The following brief list will, I hope, make clear how much added pleasure you can give to your partners at dances by truly being yourself.

If you have good teeth, be radiant.
If you are *very* thin, be serious.
If you are well developed, avoid the polka.
If you are dark, be sympathetic.
If you are blonde, be bright.

Other hints on behavior will be found in *Getting On*, *Parties*, *Conversation*, and *Friendship*; but I have one or two special reminders which I think may be useful.

If you go in a party, politeness requires you to remain in that party, however unintelligent your partners may be. But should a very dear friend who is not in your party come up and actually *ask* you to dance with him, I know you would think it unkind to refuse; and similarly, if a perfect stranger should mention his anxiety to dance with you, you know it would be discourteous even to hesitate. After all, his presence at the dance is itself a proof of his niceness (see p. 33), and, in either case, you know you are not only setting your original escort free to go off and have a drink, but are giving some other girl a quite unexpected chance to go and powder her nose in the Ladies' Cloak-room.

Should you find yourself at that old-fashioned institution, the program dance, there is one infallible way to mitigate its air of formality. By remaining in the conservatory with one of your partners during four or five dances, you can throw several unsorted couples in the ballroom into an apparent confusion which will go far to give life to the evening.

Sitting Out – It is well known that the back (or front) seat of your partner's motor provides far more opportunities for quiet conversation than any of the sitting-rooms provided indoors, where one is *all too seldom* free from the noise of the band.

Débutantes' Dances – If you are at a Débutantes' dance, you have the immense advantage that everybody knows you are nice even before you begin to prove it by your behavior. This does not, of course, absolve you from acting as always with the utmost good taste, but it does simplify some of your problems. Conversation with your partners, for instance, is limited to six questions and answers. (You may take it in turn to ask the questions, and the answers can be quite impromptu.)

1. "Isn't this a good floor?"
2. "Isn't this a good band?"
3. "What a crowd there is, isn't there?"
4. "Do you know many people?"
5. "Have you been to many other dances?"
6. "Have you seen any shows lately?"

Débutantes' dances are unlike other dances in one thing. Your behavior depends, not on what you look like, but on *who you are*. Débutantes fall into four classes:

Those so important that they prefer to be dowdy.
Those so ordinary that they have to be smart.
Those so smart that they simply *are* smart.
Those so dowdy that nothing can be done about them at all.

Your friends will soon make quite clear to you to which of these classes you belong.

Derby, The – Almost a national festival, the Derby horse-racing event takes place, not as one might have supposed at Derby, but at Epsom. In honor of it, a largish part of the population of London transfers itself to the Downs for a day's fun and a fleeting glimpse of the horses on which it has bet all its available money. A nice girl will not refuse to go even to the Derby, if she feels that by doing so she can make some deserving person happy.

First Nights – It is always jolly exciting to be present at the opening night of a new play. If your escort entertains any provincial notions of arriving at the theater punctually, you can easily make him conform to accepted usage.

Do not restrict your comments on the play from any misguided apprehension that the leading lady's relations may be sitting just in front of you. Nor should you worry if the unhappy-looking man beside you turns out to be the playwright. People who were *really* anxious to improve themselves would always be grateful for frank and unbiased criticism. Similarly, in the interval, you can have the most *intellectual* time comparing opinions with all your friends in the foyer.

Flower Show, The – Loving flowers as you do, it will be a positive pleasure for you to go to the Chelsea Flower Show with an old gentleman who is able to tell you absolutely *all* that you want to know about calceolarias, antirrhinums, and so forth. The lunch and matinée afterward you will really almost regret as tearing you away from the fascinating succession of crowded and cozy tents.

Henley – The Royal Regatta at Henley every summer is a great open-air occasion, which always attracts a vast number of spectators. You will want to dress so as to give as many people as possible the maximum amount of pleasure. To stand with the full blaze of the sunlight behind you in the Stewards' Enclosure will, if you choose your clothes carefully, show up to the full the superb transparent texture of what you have on.

If you see a boat coming with only one man in it (as is apt to occur in the case of the Diamond Sculls), you could show your interest in the proceedings by asking whether the other man has fallen into the water.

Hunt Balls – Fox-hunting, like cricket, is a national ritual as well as a national sport. Even if you do not relish the idea of fox-hunting, it should not stop you from having a jolly time at a Hunt Ball, which are usually held in the countryside. Most of the rules I have given for dances (see p. 48) apply to Hunt Balls also; but one (and a very important one) does not. At Hunt Balls *all* girls are jolly. The kind of face does not matter at all. The general atmosphere, the pink coats worn by the huntsmen, and the outbursts of merriment, will go far to bring this about automatically: but you will have to remember that the following are jokes:

Having your dress torn.
Having your feet stamped on.
Seeing your partner be sick.
Having your photograph taken while posed in the arms of somebody you detest.
Having champagne spilled over you.
Being trampled underfoot during the final gallop.
Walking through puddles in your new satin shoes.
Driving miles and miles with eight people in a four-seater car, and beginning all over again at the other end (if they have not forgotten the latch-key), before you have had time to powder your nose.

Lord's – The famous Lord's is the principal cricket ground in London, but when I refer to Lord's I really mean the Eton and Harrow schools match – one of the big events of the social as well as the cricket season – which is played here every year. This is the only occasion when you will go to watch cricket unless you are one of those people who like watching cricket (in which case, see *Cricket*). The cricket at the Eton and Harrow takes place on the large open space between the stands. You will know when it is in progress, as during that time you will not be allowed to walk about there and look at your friends. There are, however, many other places where you can walk, so this need not inconvenience you.

In the half-hour or so between your lunch interval and your tea interval you might, if your escort is an enthusiast, suggest sitting down for a few minutes and watching the game. Most people, though, are agreed that to walk up and down in the brick alley-way behind the stands, where you will not only see your friends, but feel their elbows, hat brims, parasols, heels, umbrellas, etc., at the closest possible quarters, is a far better way of getting a little fresh air between your light luncheon of salmon, iced coffee, and strawberries and your simple picnic tea of strawberries, éclairs, and iced coffee.

Remember that, unless you are very sure which people in the crowd are your escort's aunts, connections, and old family friends, it is better to be your simple and pleasant self and make only *nice* remarks about all the pretty dresses you will see there.

Night Clubs – It is well known that no nice girl ever drinks. Cocktails, sherry, the simpler red wines, the most usual white wines (such as champagne), and standard liqueurs such as Grand Marnier or brandy, cannot, however, be regarded as *drinking*. It is indiscriminate *excess* to

which people object – and very rightly, as I know you will agree. The terrible thing about drink is that it loosens not only manners but *speech*, making nice girls say things which they would otherwise never dream of saying. It is an excellent plan, if you are in a night club or some other public place, to pretend to have drunk rather more than in fact you have. You can thus say things which add considerably to the gaiety of the party, and make jokes and humorous remarks of a quite unexpected kind, with no weight on your conscience whatsoever.

Opera, The – Do not talk too loud while people are singing, for Sir Thomas Beecham does not care for it.

After you have been once to the opera you will find that the appreciation of music comes to you perfectly naturally. On your second and all subsequent visits, you have only to say that the soprano/tenor/orchestra are not up to the soprano/tenor/orchestra of the earlier evening and you will thus prove to everybody that you are a true connoisseur.

Do not, however, forget in your keenness for Art that you can give a great deal of pleasure to your friends during the intervals by making charitable yet pertinent comments upon your mutual acquaintances.

Pageants – Local pageants are frequently got up by enthusiasts in different parts of the English countryside; they will include any monarch who had any connection with the district (on horseback if the person taking the part can ride), famous local worthies in historical costume, and a scene in which the schoolchildren can perform. Everybody wants the best parts, rivalry is tremendous, and as often as not the rain pours down. It is obvious that you will not agree to take part in a pageant unless you are personally asked, in the name of friendship, by the authorities who are getting it up. This being so, you can only expect to have your altruism recognised with a part that is suited to your talents. Queen Elizabeth, Nell Gwynne, or Helen of Troy are the sort of role that immediately springs to one's mind.

If you have a part worthy of you, nothing remains for you but to be as nice to everyone as you possibly can, and to keep well away from the horses. If, however, some of the unpleasant intriguing which always goes on has robbed you of your due, you must be especially careful to show your friends how little such petty slights can move you. Be particularly nice to the girl who has got your part. Admire her clothes, congratulating her even if she has spent what you consider an ostentatious amount in her attempt to make herself presentable. You, as you can jokingly say, would of course have trusted far more to nature, and not have laid out anything like such a generous sum upon art.

If she has made herself up carelessly – perhaps, for example, putting on too much eye-black – it is of course only kind for you to tell her about it, *even* if you cannot do so until the moment when she is to take the stage.

Private Views – All important art exhibitions begin with a Private View, where you will often see some interesting people. There is *no* necessity to modify your comments if you begin to suspect that the man standing next to you painted the picture you are talking about. It will do him good to hear a little intelligent criticism.

R.A.F. Pageant, The – The Royal Air Force frequently organizes a jolly big air show to show off all their airplanes. Do not be disturbed by the noise of the planes. *They are part of the pageant*. If you come out of the mess tent for a little stroll, which many people do between lunch and tea, you will see them all flying about overhead, and any R.A.F. officer will be delighted to explain to you which is which and what they are doing.

Railway Trains – On a railway journey, as everywhere else, you will think only of others. You must, I know, have a corner seat facing the engine, but this is only because you do not want to inconvenience anybody by being sick. For the same reason, you will keep control over the heating apparatus; and if you pleasantly insist upon regulating the use of the windows, you can be sure that everyone in the carriage will have the proper amount of fresh air. (The man opposite will, however, be flattered if you invite him to do the actual *working* of the window during tunnels, etc.) You can see that your companions travel in peace by refusing to let any disturbing element (say a woman with a baby) into the compartment; and finally, should any of them appear to be really *nice* and *gentlemanly*, you might relieve the tedium of his journey considerably by entering into conversation with him and borrowing his magazines.

Recitals – Song recitals, violin recitals, piano or harp recitals at the smaller halls, are not the sort of thing you will go to unless one of your friends is the performer. If, however, your best friend is giving a recital, you must certainly go, even if she is so mean as not to give you a ticket and you have to buy one for yourself. As a matter of fact, there will be two tickets, for you will naturally want to be properly escorted. (By the way, you should either take a man whom you know you do not care about, or a man who you know cares very much about you. Recitals have sometimes a curious effect on otherwise quite sweet-natured people.) If your escort makes remarks that are unkindly critical, silence him by pointing out loudly and distinctly how brave poor So-and-so is to undertake this recital at all, and how horrid it is to criticize. She will be perfectly all right, you will add, when she has got over her nervousness. And when – as you must – you go round afterwards to congratulate your friend, do not comment upon the thinness of the audience, or on the fact that you know the hall was largely filled by the free tickets she gave to her household and acquaintances. Felicitate her upon the good attendance, and add: "After all, it is so much nicer to know that you have only your friends around you."

Regimental Dances – (See *Hunt Balls*) These annual balls, held by Army Regiments, are occasions of similar brightness and jollity, and young girls of whatever type (see *Dances*) should join whole-heartedly in the general merriment.

Restaurants – There is little to tell you about restaurants which is not a matter of simple, straightforward good manners. Remember, however, that your escort will feel insulted if you appear to calculate how much your meal is costing him, and to pick out the cheaper dishes. If you make it a rule to select the most expensive, you will be quite safe from this horrible discourtesy.

Few men are so inept that they do not know where they propose to

take you for lunch, dinner, or supper, as the case may be. Should someone appear at a loss, however, you could always suggest the Savoy, the Ritz, the Berkeley, the Carlton, or a smart restaurant of your choice, in the complete certainty that he would appreciate your unpretentious good taste.

And remember that, once there, you can make a meal go with positive *abandon* by a few sparkling comments on the curious women, and no less curious escorts, whom you and your friend will see all around you.

Tattoo, The Aldershot – The ideal remark at the Aldershot Tattoo (a very impressive display, at which hundreds of troops re-enact important military events from earlier eras) is: "It makes one think, doesn't it!" This will prove to a soldier that you love the British Empire, to a pacifist that you hate war, to an artist that you appreciate beauty, and to anyone else that you have a strong sense of humor.

The transport difficulties at the Aldershot Tattoo are acute, and if your escort is unable to return you to your home until eight o'clock the next morning, even the most suspicious-minded of parents or friends could hardly disbelieve that you had been all that time in a traffic jam.

Theaters – (See also *First Nights*) It is only polite to your escort to go to the theater in a spirit of reasonable criticism. Remarks such as the following examples would prove to him how *intelligently* you were enjoying yourself.

> "What a loathsome chorus."
>
> "No wonder they call this a farce."
>
> "How poor Amelia Stubbs has gone off."

"I *do* adore Wilberforce Wilson."

"For heaven's sake, let's go and get some fresh air."

"Of course, if we were a bit *nearer* we could easily see their expressions."

Theatricals, Amateur – Much of what I have said about *Pageants* applies also (unfortunately) to amateur theatricals. I mean that there will be a great deal of intriguing to do you out of the parts for which you are by nature and appearance fitted, and that, if you do

get such a part, there will be jealousy. However, even if you are playing lead, you will remember that it is the *team* which matters, and that loyalty to the team comes first. Should they try to cut down your part, or make you stand at the back of the stage with some other woman in front of you, you will only protest because it is for the good of the team.

If you notice any girl failing to put her back into her performance, it is your duty to say so. Do not tell her directly, or she may imagine you are being "cattish"; but mention the fact quietly to all the other members of the cast, so that it may get round to her without giving her the slightest offense. Supposing, on the night itself, some members of the cast should get more bouquets than you do yourself, you can show how much you are above any petty resentments by saying, "What a wonderful reception. The audience seems to be simply *full* of your friends."

Weddings – (See *Cause and Effect*, p. 141)

Weekends – (See *Staying with People*, p. 77)
But remember that weekends are divided into three kinds.

(1) Country or country-house, which everyone goes on.

(2) Provincial, which you will not go on, but which are recognized to exist.

(3) A kind about which no nice girl knows anything whatsoever.

Wimbledon – Your escort will be charmed by your originality and appreciation if you say to him after watching some spirited play on the Centre Court: "It makes me feel I shall never play tennis again." You will almost certainly find that the style and grace of the men players makes them better worth watching than the women (admirable, in their way, though these are), and, this being so, the best time to suggest tea to your escort is during the progress of a Ladies' Singles or Doubles match.

Zoological Gardens, The – It is unlikely that you will go to the zoo except to give pleasure to a small boy and perhaps to the uncle who accompanies him. But if you should go, your love of children will remind you that your charge will be far happiest if allowed to roam about entirely by himself. A shilling to buy sweets (which his uncle will readily provide) will make him even happier, and he is not at all *likely* to make himself sick.

An amusing game can be played by likening the various birds, reptiles, and animals to your mutual acquaintances, but I think you will both find that the shady seats in sequestered alleys, where one can talk at ease upon topics however serious, are the best place to await the return of your fortunate and indulged little charge.

2. ESCORTS

In the above guide to Public Occasions, I have naturally assumed that on each appearance you are with a suitable escort. It does occasionally happen, though, that you have to appear on some public occasion with an escort who is not what you would have chosen at all. One hears, for instance, of girls going to dances with a schoolboy brother, to the opera with a female friend, or to Lord's with elderly clergymen. I am not suggesting that you would do these things, or anything like them; but the whole question of suitable escorts is one about which you can hardly reflect too much.

You want, do you not, to be kind to people? Well, is it kind, I ask you seriously, to go about in public with an escort so unsuitable that his comparison with you will occasion remarks that are in no way to his credit? It is not your reputation, I know, that you will think about. It is the remarks which will inevitably be caused by such a person's appearance in company so obviously above him. Should it happen, then, that an Australian sheep-farmer wants to take you to Ascot, or a worthy but uncultured provincial acquaintance to the restaurant frequented by all your intimate friends, you will I am sure take the only kind course of action. Tell him you have a headache, or that Ascot bores you, or that you have

promised to go to your Infant Welfare center that day, or any polite excuse that occurs to you. He would thank you, if he only knew.

Certain escorts, however, even if they seem unsuitable, can very well be tolerated. You want to be kind to as many people as possible. If, for instance, an artistic, but otherwise gentlemanly young man should want to take you to the Horse Show, do not refuse. He may know nothing about horses, and may make the most *foolish* remarks; but a little laugh, showing him that you think he is clever and your friends near by that you think him a fool, will soon put everyone at ease. Similarly, if an opulent but boorish friend of your father's asks you to his box at the opera, there is no need at all to refuse him, as long as he does not suck his teeth. After all, even if you do suffer a little uneasiness in their company, one thought should sustain you. Not only are you being kind to them; you can give immense pleasure to your other friends the next day by telling them all your adventures.

And one last reminder. There are some men so nondescript that they can only be described by the inelegant term "wet." These, no less than nice people, will be anxious for your company. Why should you refuse them? (Though on this, see p. 30.) If you give them the privilege of escorting you to a party, it is perfectly possible that you will there meet someone so nice, and so much in need of your friendship, that your unselfish action in going will be more than justified. As long as you make it quite clear to the dull young man that you are only going with him because it strikes you as comic, that he need *never*, on any account, expect you to repeat your kindness a second time, and that your opinion of him mingles amusement with a certain legitimate disgust, more good than harm may be done by this charitable departure from your usual course.

3. Culture

I have put this important question under *Public Occasions* as you will not, except with *very* rare people, have any need for it on private ones (see p. 88). Culture, as I have said before, is a difficult problem. You do not want to be like those unhappy girls who have nothing better to talk about; but you *do* want to prove yourself brilliant and well informed if people start talking about culture and you cannot distract their attention.

The following index covers *the entire range of culture*. With the two lists of names which follow, it gives all the things that you need to know and exactly what to know about them. To learn any more would stamp you at once as pedantic. In *An Index to Culture*, I have gone so far as to give you *two* remarks on some of the outstanding topics. This may seem excessive, but there is no harm in learning them both. Then, if the first remark does not fully impress your hearer with your depth and originality, the second is almost certain to reduce him to an awestruck silence.

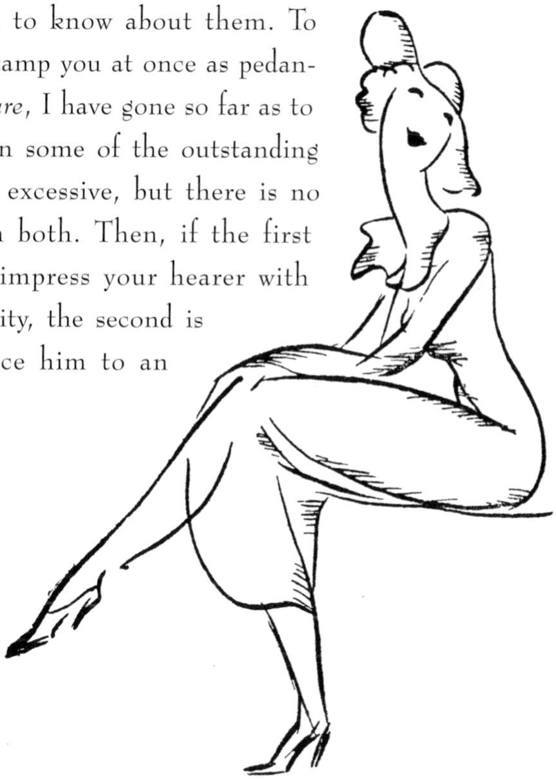

AN INDEX TO CULTURE

Academy, The Royal – "It's not up to last year."

Art – "It makes one think, somehow."
"I do adore art, don't you?"

Ballet – "The *décor* is shoddy."
"I do adore ballet, don't you?"

Classics, Any – "Don't talk to me about the classics."
"I do adore classics, don't you?"

Music – "Music is the great international language."
"I do adore music, don't you?"

Novels – "There's nothing worth reading nowadays."

Opera – "I never can think how they do it."
"I do adore music, don't you?"

Pictures – "It's almost as good as a photograph."
"I do adore pictures, don't you?"

Plays, Serious – "Unhealthy, I call it."

Poetry – "I do love nice poetry. I used to know 'If' by heart."

Politics – See separate index.

Statues, Any – "That reminds me of one of my cousins."

Wireless – "It's wonderful, when you think of it."
"I do adore music, don't you?"

Sub-index I

PEOPLE YOU OUGHT TO KNOW ABOUT

There comes a time in every girl's life when someone asks her "What do you think about So-and-so?"' and *she does not know who they are talking about*. It is to obviate this horrible dilemma that the following list has been made. I have not included people whom you know about already, such as the Prince of Wales or Bing Crosby; but everyone else of any importance will be found here, and about anyone who is not included you can safely and rightly say "Oh, So-and-so? I've never heard of him." A star denotes that the person is handsome. A dagger means "modern."

Beecham, Sir Thomas – Conducts operas.
Doesn't like people to talk.
**Coward, Noël* – Writes plays.
†*Einstein* – Does mathematics.
†*Eliot, T. S.* – Writes modern poetry.
†*Epstein* – Did "Genesis."
†*Freud* – Wrote a book about dreams.
Galsworthy – Wrote a book called *The Forsyte Saga*.
Inge, Dean – A dean.
†*Lawrence, D. H.* – *Not the same* as Lawrence of Arabia.
**Nichols, Beverley* – A gardener.
Priestley – Wrote *The Good Companions*.
Shaw, Bernard – Wrote plays.
**Walpole, Hugh* – Writes classics.
**Wells, H. G.* – Writes classics.

Sub-index II

POLITICS

Politics change so much that it is not safe to make any remark about them unless you have taken it out of *The Times* leader for the day. All you can do is know which people are of which nationality, and consequently which ones to respect. I hope that the following list will help you.

British – Mr. Anthony Eden, Mr. Baldwin, Mr. Hore-Belisha, Mr. Ramsay Macdonald, Mr. Lloyd George.

Foreign – President Roosevelt. All Frenchmen.

Dictators – Hitler, Mussolini, Sir Oswald Moseley, and Sir Stafford Cripps.

An intelligent smile at the mention of the above names will stamp you at once as a keen observer of modern political problems.

4. Parties

PARTIES

A party is a gathering of people whose only ambition is to give pleasure to one another. You may hear ill-bred people give other reasons for attendance at parties, such as:

that they like their hosts;
that they hate their hosts;
that they like the food, the wine, the river, or the private golf-course;
that they had to fill in the time somehow;
that relations had called on them;
that they want to meet So-and-so;
that they want a free meal;
that they couldn't get out of it.

These things, for such people, may very well be true; but your own conscience is clear. You go to parties purely from a high sense of duty.

Parties are of so many kinds that it is impossible to list them all. *Any* gathering of really nice people with unselfish aims is in point of fact a party, and to your conduct at these you will want to devote quite as much attention as you give to Public Occasions – if not, indeed, rather more. All Public Occasions, of course, mean a party; Ascot, dances, Henley, Lord's, etc. Your behavior on these occasions you already know. I am here concerned with the smaller, less public functions where you are among your own circle with no jostling onlookers; where the spirit of mutual friendship can be relied upon; and where, if you set about it rightly and choose appreciative people, you can lay the foundations of more kindness and help than anywhere else.

Broadly speaking, parties fall under the following heads:

Cocktail parties.
Dinner parties.
Garden parties.
House parties.
Housewarming parties.
Lunch parties.
Picnic parties.
Restaurant parties.
Sherry parties.
Supper parties.
Swimming parties.
Tea parties.
Theater parties.

This list is not – and could not be – exhaustive. There are as many kinds of parties as there are people with the good taste to give them. But it does not matter. I need give you no specific instruction about how to behave at each species of party, for *you behave just the same at them all*. And that behavior, like all your behavior, can be summed up in the two words which express your unfailing ideal: BE NICE.

Here, however, are certain general observations which I think you may find helpful.

You will *always* thank your host or hostess before going away from

their party. After all, they have taken a great deal of trouble, and if the results are, shall we say, not outstanding, that is their misfortune rather than their fault. It is nice, if you can, to mention some special reason why you have enjoyed yourself. For example:

"How clever of you to have kept your numbers so small. I've never had room to move about at a party before."

"It was *such* a success, my dear. Nobody got in the least bit drunk."

"Such a magnificent noise, my dears – I never heard a single word that anybody said."

"Those sandwiches were delicious – the *whole plateful* was gone in a minute."

"It's so nice to get a chance to talk to all one's old schoolfriends."

"A *delightful* evening, Henry – so *restful*."

Or, at the conclusion of a weekend party, you could say:

"It *has* been fun. It seems ages and ages since Friday."

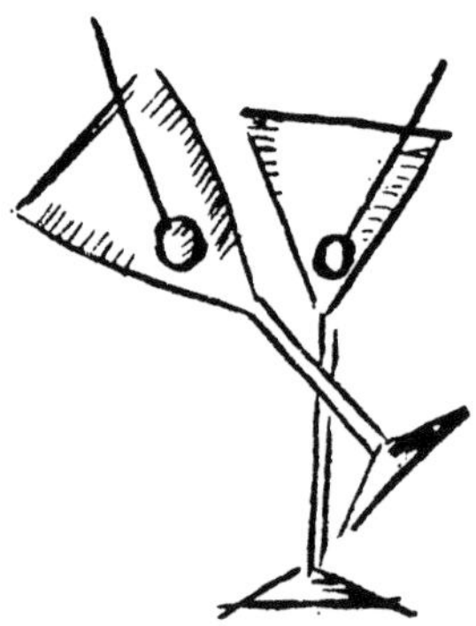

STAYING WITH PEOPLE

House parties, weekend parties, shooting parties, and visits are all different aspects of *staying with people*, and apart from the necessity of talking about shooting at shooting parties the same behavior will be adequate for them all. Remember that you have certain duties in return for the kindness of your hosts in having you (even though, in actual fact, the cost of your food is *negligible* and they make no other outlay on you at all). You have to help with the general entertainment; to seek out and enliven men who seem lonely or unhappy (see p. 124); to reassure nervous young girls who are uneasy about their clothing or appearance; to prevent intrigue or any departure from the conventions; and in general to be *kind* and *nice*. The following notes will I think help you.

If you come upon a man who is looking unhappy, you might well say: "I feel like that, too. For heaven's sake, let's get out and go for a walk."

Or: "They're *such* kind people, in theory."

Or: "It's not long now till Monday."

To young girls you will be as kind as you know how to be, realizing what torments of nervousness they are apt to endure. If, for example, they come down to breakfast in the wrong sort of dress – a cotton dress, shall we say, when everyone else is in tweeds – do not comment upon it directly. Some little oblique remark can bring the error home to them much more kindly. For instance:

"If it had only been warmer today, we might almost have got our cotton frocks out."

"What wonderful sunshine. I longed to come down in a cotton dress, but I knew very well what you men would all say."

Any remark like this will not fail to send the grateful girl simply scurrying off to change the minute she has finished her breakfast.

It may well happen that the last night of your stay sees you wearing a new evening dress while this *unfortunate* girl, owing to some negligence, is wearing an old one over again. Go out of your way to show her how little you think such things matter. You might say, for example:

"What a *sweet* dress, my dear. I think you're so wise to go on and on wearing it."

"I believe someone *asked* you to put on that dress again!"

"I wish I had your courage, Daphne darling."

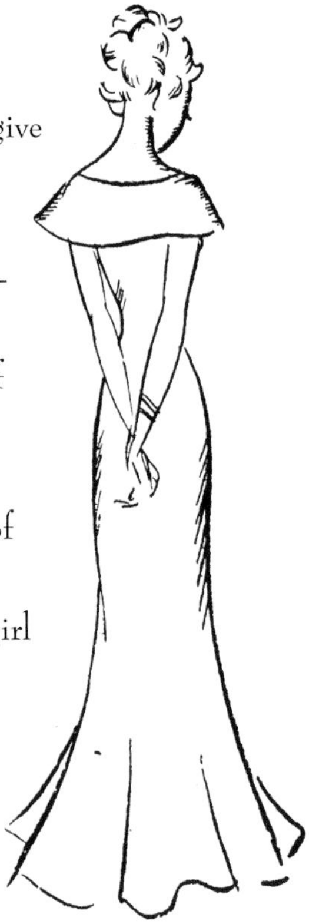

And if she should ask you – as she well may – to give your opinion of some outfit, give her the little reassurance she is longing for. It will make so much difference to her, and you can do it quite well without being dishonest if you say, for example:

"Very pretty, my dear – and after all, it's not as if people *noticed* what you have on."

For other courtesies to your hosts, see *Parties* (p. 73), and *Invitations* (p. 79). For consideration of their staff, see *Kindness to Others* (p. 111), and *Situations* (p. 127). For other suitable remarks to girl friends who are fellow-guests see *Clothes, Other People's* (p. 20), and *Kindness: to Women* (p. 107). For further ways of helping the lonely or unhappy see *Kindness*, *Conversation* (throughout), *Friendship*, *Affection*, and *Sympathy*.

INVITATIONS

Generally speaking, it is better to be invited to parties. This can be managed in several ways, the easiest of which is simply to know nice hospitable people and see that they do not forget you. It is often worthwhile to be polite to people whom you would not ordinarily bother about at all, if you know that they often give parties and are longing to be on friendly enough terms with you to invite you to them. For weekend parties, or house parties, much the kindest thing is to invite yourself. Hostesses will be delighted to find that you treat them so informally, and a telegram dispatched as you take the train, informing them that you will arrive at lunch-time, will save them the bother of having to reply. For dinner parties this method is less effective; but a word in season reminding a friend of yours how much you are longing to meet Mr. So-and-so or Lord Blank can hardly fail to be welcome and to have its effect. It is often especially nice to say that you want to meet a certain *woman* – Miss Whoever it is, or Mrs. Dash from Yorkshire. This marks you off as one of those really charming young girls who are as nice to their own sex as they are to the other.

For any informal parties, such as cocktail parties, sherry parties, and housewarming parties, it is friendly to dispense with an invitation altogether. The man who takes you into his friends' houses would obviously not do so unless he were sure of your welcome, and any apparent coldness on the part of the hostess can easily be excused on the grounds of momentary surprise.

If you should hear of a party to which by some odd oversight you have not been invited, I do not suggest that you should *go*. You should simply arrive at your friend's house at the time it is to be given, dressed in clothes that make it quite clear you had not expected to come upon such festivities (but which happen to be unobtrusively suitable). They will be overjoyed to see you, and will of course invite you to join them. If the party in question is given by a man you thought nice and includes girls about whom you can only be charitable, quite an interesting conversation may be held. (This however, verges upon *Advanced Instruction*, see p. 123.) If it is given by a girl friend of yours who has *purposely* forgotten to invite you out of sheer spite and jealousy, you can say to her: "Darling, I *know* it was only an accident," and she will quite understand that you forgive her.

HELPING WITH A PARTY

In this I might include "Giving a Party," were it not for two obvious considerations. One is that any parties you give will be arranged at this stage of your life by your elders, and all you have to do is to keep yourself perfectly fresh for the occasion by resting as much as you can beforehand and not taxing your strength in domestic preparations. If in addition you see that all the nice men present have ample opportunities of talking to you, their hostess, you will have done all that can possibly be expected of you. Women guests who eye you with apparent reproach will do so only because they are unable to hide their jealousy.

But it is not the part of a young girl's duty to give hospitality. You can give far more pleasure by going round to the parties of other people, by making them a success with your looks, your wit, and your charm of manner, than you could by toiling at home over catering, lists of names, and so forth. If you were plain and dull and felt that

your presence at parties was a burden, then might be the time to think of attempting some return. As things are, you know that the debts of hospitality are amply discharged by your consenting to be present at a party at all.

Helping with a party, though, is another matter. If a dear friend of yours (a young married woman, perhaps, or one of those courageous girls who work all day for their living) is giving a party, nothing could be nicer than for you to go along and give her the benefit of your help and advice.

You can, for example, give her hints about the catering. You will want to show that you are considering her pocket; so, when you bring some special sweet or wine to her notice, it would be kind and thoughtful to say "I know you'll like it – it's nice and cheap."

Do not be critical of her lack of accommodation. Say: "But how heavenly. We'll be *right* on top of each other," as if there were nothing you liked better than being crowded to death.

Nor, of course, should you criticize her list of guests. You will see some names that you know, and can truthfully say "Well, thank goodness he's coming, anyway." And if you ask her "Darling, who *are* all these people?" she will of course tell you readily.

Moreover, when the party is in progress you will be able to consider yourself as quite one of the family. You can of course retain enough independence to tell your friends jokingly what *fun* you had with the preparations, what difficulty you had in persuading dear old So-and-so that she must buy good sherry, and so on, and so on; but you will be able to be of help to your hostess in a dozen unobtrusive ways. If, for instance, you see her talking to some people with such animation that she is forgetting her duty to others, the kindest thing to do is to make a gesture indicating that her vest is showing or her shoulder-strap slipping down her arm. This will recall her to herself at once.

5. YOUR ELDERS

The whole question of behavior to your elders is one that may well be regarded as vexed. Naturally you would like nothing better than always to be polite to them; but the following difficulties, as you will find, insist on being taken into account.

Your elders are old-fashioned.

They do not understand the rising generation.

They do not try to.

They think they know best.

They object to perfectly ordinary behavior, such as, for example, staying out to dinner without letting them know.

They talk too much.

Last, and most comprehensive, they are hopelessly narrow-minded.

These faults are obvious to everybody except themselves, and you will of course have no scruples about pointing them out to them, even though you know that the hope of reform is practically non-existent.

But here arises the *universal* difficulty. Elders, as we have said, are narrow-minded. If you attempt to point out their shortcomings, or even to go your own way and take as little notice of them as possible, they are apt to retaliate in the unfairest possible manner. Not only will they talk to you a great deal about what *they* consider *your* failings. This you could bear, for you are used to it and do not even need to listen. What is far worse, they may attempt to curtail the pleasures, as they call them, which are not only your right but your necessity. They may forbid you to go to certain parties. They may take it into their heads to disapprove of some man who you know very well is nice, and forbid you to see him anymore. They may refuse to put up for the night some completely charming person whom you have asked to escort you to an important dance. They may prove irrevocably unwilling to organize any little pleasures for you at all. Further questions even, such as dress allowances, traveling money, and the right to be waited on by your mother's maid, are hopelessly in their power. In fact, owing to the utter unfairness of the whole system, they have everything their own way.

What then must you do? The answer is clear. You must apply to this problem also your unvarying rule. You must *be nice*. You will consider their feelings, and conceal from their knowledge any facts which would give them unhappiness, or any anxieties which would arouse quite needless anxiety. You will always point out their faults as gently as possible. You will even keep out of their way, realizing that if they have *any* sensibilities they could only be made unhappy by continual evidence of the unbridgeable gulf between you. You will in fact, in the face of whatever injustice and provocation, be *just as nice to your elders as you would be to anybody else*.

THE NICE GIRL'S GUIDE

PART III
PRIVATE OCCASIONS

This book takes life in the order in which you will come to it. First, *Beginning*: learning to make the most of yourself for the sake of others, and getting to know people who will value your thoughtfulness. Second, *Public Occasions*, upon which you increase the circle of really nice people whom it is your one ambition to help. Third, and most important of all, come *Private Occasions*.

Private Occasions represent your supreme chance of doing good to other people. Once you have ascertained that a friend is nice (see p. 33), Private Occasions will almost inevitably follow, and it is then that your responsibilities begin. You have to know, above everything else, what to *say* to him, and for this reason the greater part of the following section is devoted to *Conversation*. A short chapter on *Kindness* will guide your natural impulses into their most profitable channels, and some further hints on *Presents* may perhaps be of use. Finally, as we do not nowadays blink the fact that one thing may lead to another, I conclude the section with a short synopsis of *Love*.

1. CONVERSATION

RANGE

The range of conversation is practically unlimited. From the moment when you begin to know a man *at all*, the following topics will inevitably arise from your mutual sympathy, and you will find that between them they cover all that you could ever want to say or have said to you, and give the *utmost* scope for your sympathy, wit, and intelligence.

Him.
You.
His looks.
Your looks.
The moon.
The sun.
The cinema.
His past experiences.
Your past experiences.
Hot rhythm.
Your elders.
Sport.
Motors.
Airplanes.
Your clothes.
Other girls' clothes.
Mickey Mouse.
Life.

There are certain people of limited tastes who *from choice* include in Private Conservation talk about books, history, geography, and other branches of what is generally described as *Culture* (see *Culture*). Anyone who does so in your presence shows a grave lack of human understanding (compare *Taxis*), and it is unlikely that you will ever feel any strong mutual sympathy.

POLITENESS

The secret of happy conversation is unfailing politeness. Do not think of yourself. Think all the time of your friend and what he is feeling. Think what he *needs*, what he *hopes*, what he *expects* of you. Say what is *best* for him, at no matter what cost to yourself. Politeness like this outweighs all conventional brilliance. The following examples will show what I mean. They cover many occasions, and many different gradations of friendship.

Q. "Oh, look what's coming. She's my sister-in-law."
A. "Never mind. Here is a taxi."

Q. "People tell me I'm getting in a groove."
A. "I will help you to get out of it."

Q. "I'm supposed to be going to stay with some poisonous people."
A. "You cannot do that. It is extension night at Quaglino's. Telegraph that you have a chill on your liver."

Q. "I think you are beautiful."
A. "Oh, look. Here come six fire engines."

Q. "I think you are beautiful."
A. "Do you – "

Q. The modern girl is beyond me."
A. "I am not a modern girl."

Q. "Modern girls are so wonderful."
A. "Darling – "

Q. "I am so unhappy."
A. "Life is indeed a problem for the sensitive."

Q. "I am so unhappy."
A. "You should take more exercise."

Q. "What shall I do about my overdraft?"
A. "You need a new car."

Q. "Did I ever tell you about my great-grandfather?"
A. "I have an appointment with the hairdresser."

Q. "It is very hot."
A. "Sit here beside me, in order that you may become cool."

Q. "It is very hot."
A. "Why do you not summon the waiter?"

Q. "I am as broad-minded as anyone."
A. "Oh, do you think so?"

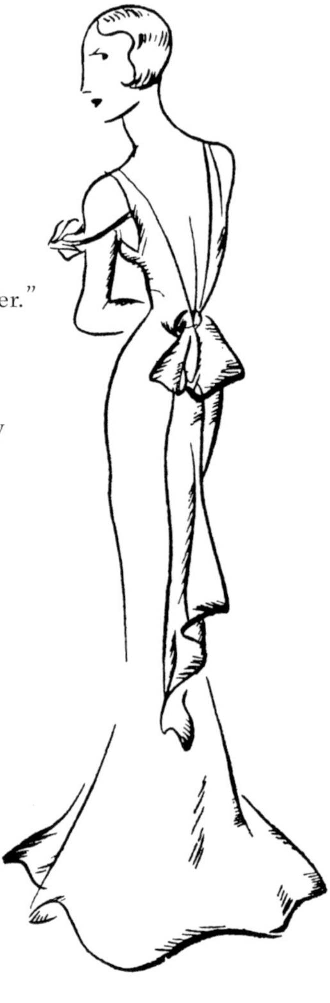

TAXIS

Conversation in taxis runs along certain well-established lines which you will rapidly discover for yourself. One hint only I will give you. Distrust men who spend their time during a taxi ride discussing the weather or giving imitations of goldfish, saxophones, etc. They show a lack of serious purpose.

THE TELEPHONE

The telephone plays so important a part in modern life that it is essential for you to be perfectly at home with it. The chief difficulties, you will find, are *opening remarks* and *good-byes*. Conversation in between is comparatively simple (see *General Notes*); but beginning and ending can cause serious anxiety to the unprepared.

Beginning – If you are summoned to the telephone and told "Mr. So-and-so to speak to you," there is, of course, nothing to be done but to say "Hullo" (see, however, *Hullos*). If you answer the telephone yourself, though, and recognise (shall we say) John speaking, there are several courses open to you.

(1) Say "Oh, *Charlie*!" in tones of delight.

(2) Say "Who is speaking, please?"

(3) Say "Hullo, darling" (see, however, *Terms of Endearment*).

(4) Say "Oh, it's you, is it?"

Hullos – The word "Hullo" can express as many shades of meaning as a whole bookful of poetry. With a little practice you can easily make it convey any of the following complex and varied sentiments.

"Oh, *there* you are. I've been longing to hear you for hours."

"Yes? Yes? I'll be as patient as I can, but I warn you – "

"You of all people? What a heavenly surprise."

"You? Oh, lord."

"This is Miss Carruthers speaking, and don't you forget it."

"How jolly it is to hear you. I am, of course, completely unsentimental about you, but all the same it's delightful to talk to one's friends."

"I know people regard you as a bit of a joke, but I assure you it gives me real pleasure to talk to you, and I think you're sweet."

Ending – A nice girl will *never* suggest that she wants to see her friend. To do so, she knows, would be vulgar and grasping. It would give him an exaggerated idea of his own importance. It would rank her with those gold digging creatures whose one aim it is to have a good time at somebody else's expense. It would, in fact, be *entirely* out of character. She will avoid it, and confine herself to a simple, unstudied "good-bye."

This does not mean, of course, that she will not *consider* him. Knowing as she does how badly her friend wants to be permitted to see her, she will always contrive to slip in some helpful remark in the course of their conversation. For example:

"I've got absolutely nothing to do on Tuesday."
"See you soon then, my pet?"
"When do we meet again, darling?"
"I hear there's a wonderful play at the Lyric."
"How is your car getting on?"

These combine friendship with perfect dignity, and any man who is nice (see *How to Know Nice People*) will eagerly grasp the hope they hold out to him.

Good-Byes – The word "good-bye", like the word "hullo", can express many shades of feeling which the nice girl would not venture to put into actual speech. The following are some of its commoner meanings, and she should lose no time in learning up the various tones which convey them.

"Till Tuesday, then. But please don't suppose that I really mind twopence whether I see you again or not."

"Till tonight, then – Oh, darling … . "

"Good-bye for the present, Mr. Smithers."

"I'm sure you mean well, but I *am* in a hurry."

"I should never have suspected, when we began this conversation, what an extraordinary affinity there was between us."

"It's a pity you had to say all this, I think; but if you should ever repent of your base suspicions, you will not find me wholly deaf to entreaty."

"Have you *really* finished – "

"All right, all right – I'm in just as much of a hurry as you are."

General Notes – Telephone conversation is much the same as ordinary conversation (see *Range*). Owing, however, to the fact that the talkers are separated, it tends to become a little more *abstract* and *general* than talk between people who can see and (as it were) touch one another. Telephone conversation may be said to fall into the following classes:

Invitations.
Narrative or anecdote.
Intelligent criticism of mutual friends.

A few examples will, I think, make clear what extensive opportunities these classes provide both for brilliance and sympathy.

Invitations – The nice girl is grateful for invitations, if they are entirely considerate and suitable, and she does not hesitate to accept them (see, however, *How to Know Nice People*). After all, they prove that her attempts to be *kind* and *sympathetic* have not entirely failed in their object, and give her further opportunities of living up to her ideals. The following remarks would show both formal gratitude and a certain originality.

"My dear, how superb."
"My sweet, how exciting."
"Darling, how divine."

Anecdotes – All nice girls are wonderful listeners. To stories of speed-limits exceeded, golf matches won, trains missed, parents outwitted, or parties endured, you could reply with brilliant suitability and appreciation:

"My dear, how superb."
"My sweet, how exciting."
"Darling, how divine."

Criticism – No nice girl is *ever* unkindly censorious. This does not, however, mean that she should not make intelligent use of her critical abilities. A thorough examination of the characters of her friends will be of the greatest benefit both to her and to the person who helps her to make it. If your friend tells you stories about them that are *new* and *revealing*, remarks such as the following will prove how completely you take them to heart.

"My dear, how superb."
"My sweet, how exciting."
"Darling, how divine."

Making Calls – The nice girl seldom has to make calls for herself, for once her character is understood people are only too anxious to ring her up whenever they possibly can. There are times, however, when her kindness of heart will literally force her to dial the number of some particular friend. These occasions fall into two groups.

A. Reassurance – If a particular friend has not telephoned you for over a week, this can mean one thing only. He is modest; *he is afraid of being a nuisance*. Common courtesy insists that you should ring him up and reassure him.

The introductory remark needs some care. It is best and kindest to say "I believe you'd forgotten all about me!" This, while light and humorous, has an undercurrent of thoughtfulness which gives him no choice but to make the answer he is anxious to make.

Some men are so boorish and unreasonable that *they do not like you to ring them up at their office*. There are various ways of dealing with such discourtesy, but I dare say you will feel that the truest kindness is to go on ringing them up *as much as you possibly can*, in the hope that you may reform them.

B. Consideration – Should it ever occur that you feel lonely, apprehensive, or temporarily misunderstood, do not be selfish about it, and stay all day moping by yourself. *Ring your friend up*. Allow him to take you to the theater, or out to dinner, or to arrange any other form of consolation that his good nature suggests. He would never forgive you if you did not permit him this small chance of proving his friendship and esteem.

If you have rung up a friend six or seven times, and each time, when you have greeted him, the connection is *immediately* cut off, you may begin to suspect that he is purposely avoiding you. In such a case you must instantly write to him pointing out that he is not worthy of you and that you do not intend ever to see him again, no matter how much he pesters you.

GRACE

Conversation – even brilliant conversation – is often ruined by lack of grace on the part of the speaker. Nothing is so striking as a graceful attitude. It adds point to your wit, and depth to your sympathy. It is extraordinary how many girls fail to realize this. I have known otherwise intelligent girls who received men's confidences while seated upright on a dining-room chair, or offered their own while standing smoking in front of an uncurtained window.

The following attitudes are infallibly graceful:

Lying back against the cushions of a car with your face upturned (if it is fine) to the open heavens.

Reclining in a chair with comfortable arms. It is a pretty gesture to stretch one leg unconsciously out in front of you and slowly move your foot about.

Lying on a hearth-rug is charming and unstudied for those with attractive figures.

But the best of all is to fling yourself thoughtlessly on a sofa, and stretch out your arms.

You will find that, such is the influence of a graceful attitude, your friend will instantly adopt one which is the perfect complement to your own.

TERMS OF ENDEARMENT

The nice girl will follow prescribed social usage in the matter of addressing her friends. I need hardly add that this does not mean you should keep on calling them "Mister". It means quite the reverse. Owing to the exceptional beauty of the relation between the sexes to-day, it is customary to use the term "darling" at the earliest possible moment. To fail in this would mark you at once as uncultured. "My dear" should also be used with the greatest freedom: but it must be remembered that the more friendly you become with a man, the more careful you are not to be vulgarly demonstrative. The following table, giving greetings for the same friend at five different stages of your acquaintance, will I hope make this clear:

1st stage. "Darling, how *heavenly*."

2nd stage. "My dear, what a joke."

3rd stage. "Hullo, Tom."

4th stage. "Oh, it's you, is it?"

5th stage. "Hullo, you great hulking lunatic."

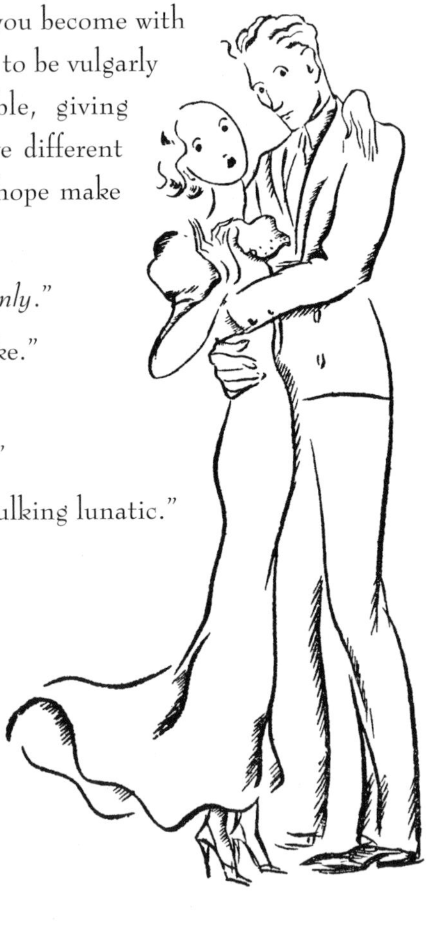

ADJECTIVES

Nothing proves your wit and intelligence better than a brilliant array of adjectives. Philosophy, sympathy, criticism, scorn, and appreciation can all be expressed by adjectives. The wise girl is never at a loss for one: and the following list, if committed to memory, will provide her with scintillating comments on every aspect of life.

There are of course adjectives that express less *whole-hearted* approval than those mentioned above: "beastly," for example, and some that are even stronger in their condemnation. For the use of these, see *Language*.

JOKES

The really nice girl has not a trace of vulgarity in her nature. She is thus rather exercised to know *which jokes to laugh at* and which not to understand. In public, of course – at revues and so forth – it is best to laugh only at the simpler forms of humor, such as misplaced whitewash and jokes about Aberdeen; but if you slip away occasionally to those places with a girlfriend whose idea of fun is the same as your own, this rule can suitably be neglected. At parties, when one of your friends tells a story which you frankly regard as in doubtful taste, it is wise to laugh only if the other girls do, and then rather *less* than they do. This will stamp you at once as the purest-minded girl in the gathering. *Never* on any account give an instant bellow of laughter before you have seen what the others are going to do. Bellows of laughter are vulgar in any case.

In private, the appreciation of jokes is governed first and foremost by consideration for others. It is the same golden rule as applies to everything else that you do or say. What is your friend like? What does he most want you to be like? When you have answered these questions, nothing remains but to satisfy him. You will make yourself happy in doing so.

Some men imagine that a funny story is, shall we say, an account of how they missed the morning train to the city. If they tell you a story like this, do not fail in politeness. Laugh when they expect you to (the point will be marked by their first laughing themselves), and you will prove to them how fully you live up to their ideal of womanhood.

But it is with really intelligent humor that your chief difficulties will arise. Most men – one might almost say all men – enjoy intelligent humor, but *they do not think that you have the right sort of mind for it*. In fact, owing to some strange masculine perversion, they prefer you not to have. This you must on no account *ever* forget. If it pleases them to feel superior, to suppose that you cannot understand the funny side of life – well, there it is; you would not wish it otherwise. You must do your best, and, should they try to prove their superiority by telling you a really funny story, you must laugh politely, but with such obvious lack of enjoyment that they will be sure you have not seen the point. (And if indeed you have not, any of your girlfriends would willingly explain it to you afterward.)

When you are on terms of real friendship with a man, matters become slightly easier – by which I mean only, of course, that it is easier to be perfectly unselfish in the matter of pleasing him. Most men take a pleasure in educating any girl they are fond of (see p. 24). Your friend will almost certainly give you a progressive course of what we might call standard English humor, and will be delighted to discover how readily, step by step, you respond to it. (Some men, by the way, prefer to delay this course until after marriage, but this you will soon discover from their general conversation.) One point, though, is of vital importance. If you make a new friend, *do not suppose* that your training with him can go on from the point where your last friend left it. He would not like it. He wants to educate you right from the beginning himself.

LANGUAGE

It is well known that no nice girl ever swears. She has, however, an unselfish horror of making other people unhappy by appearing frigid or prudish. Should this appear likely, she will go out of her way to venture some picturesque expression that will put them all at their ease.

She will, of course, remain quite unmoved if a man uses forceful language while she is with him. Even the most gentlemanly people do not always confine themselves to conventional epithets, and a certain picturesqueness may be taken as a sign of manliness. And should a friend wish to educate her in some of the richer Old English phrases (compare *Jokes*), she will prove her affection and thoughtfulness best by learning all that he has to teach her.

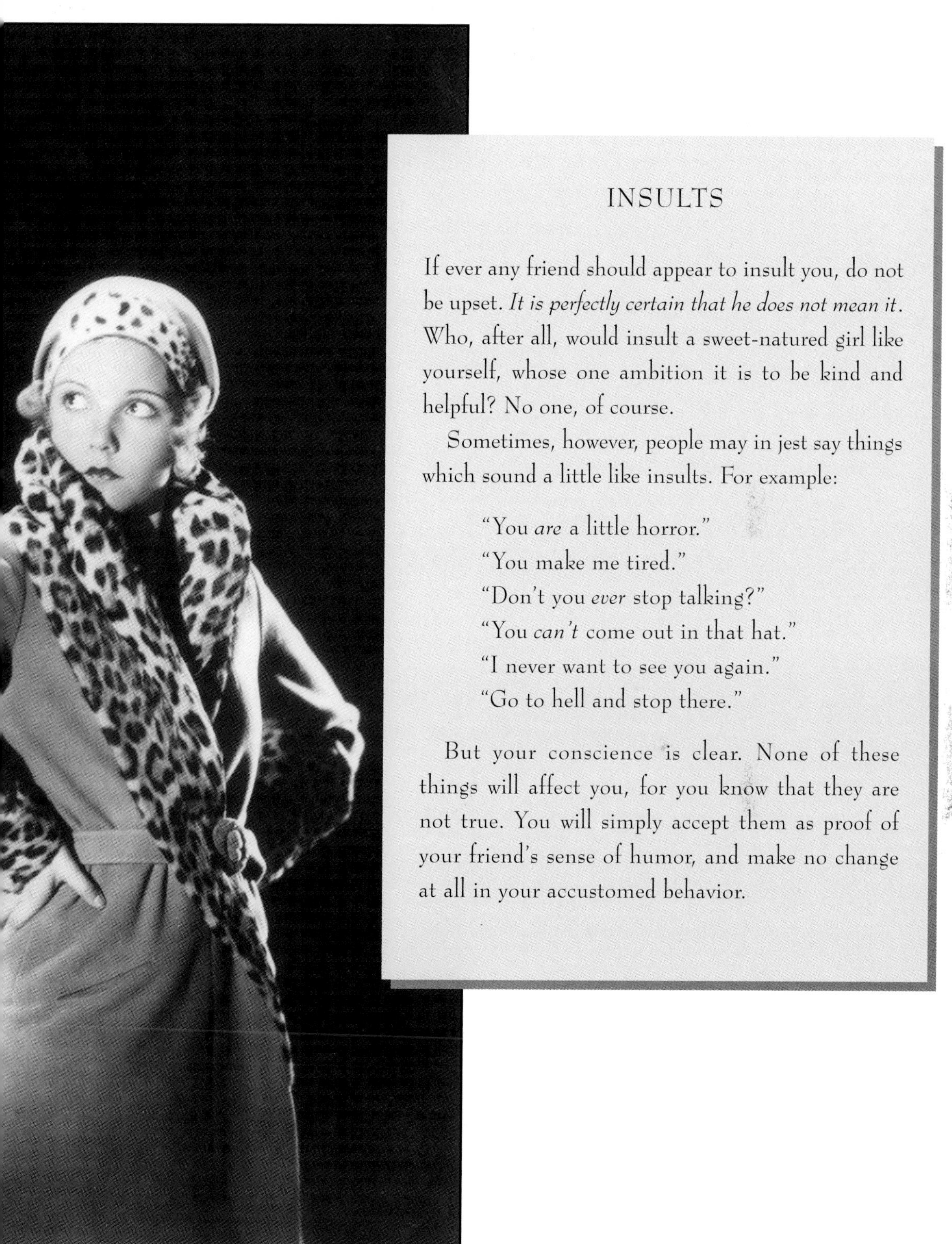

INSULTS

If ever any friend should appear to insult you, do not be upset. *It is perfectly certain that he does not mean it*. Who, after all, would insult a sweet-natured girl like yourself, whose one ambition it is to be kind and helpful? No one, of course.

Sometimes, however, people may in jest say things which sound a little like insults. For example:

> "You *are* a little horror."
> "You make me tired."
> "Don't you *ever* stop talking?"
> "You *can't* come out in that hat."
> "I never want to see you again."
> "Go to hell and stop there."

But your conscience is clear. None of these things will affect you, for you know that they are not true. You will simply accept them as proof of your friend's sense of humor, and make no change at all in your accustomed behavior.

2. KINDNESS

TO MEN

When one is young one does not always, even with the best will in the world, know what is real kindness and what is not. A thing which you might consider nice for somebody may in reality be not good for him *at all*. The few remarks I have set down here for your guidance will, I think, help you to be kind only in the ways which are *fundamentally* best for *everyone*.

You might think, for example, that the kindest thing for somebody you are fond of is to praise him, to encourage him, to let him have his own way upon all occasions. But *this is not so*. You do not want to be responsible for spoiling a person's character. The following remarks, though at first sight a little informal, are far truer examples of kindness than any amount of unreasoning adulation.

"Yes, I'll come, if you like. I've nothing better to do."
"One has to suppose that you do your best."
"Now George is my idea of a *really* handsome man."
"You *must* think I'm hard up for amusement."
"You do make me laugh."
"I wish you played tennis like Henry."
"No one can say you're *impetuous*."
"You'd pass almost *anywhere*, darling."

Similarly, if you are out with anybody, it is often kind to break down all formalities from the very beginning, and talk to all the other friends whom you meet *just as if he was not there*.

But the kindest thing you can do for a man is to give him free exercise for his natural generosity and affection. You, I know, have done what you could for him without any thought of reward; but he will want to show his gratitude in tangible as well as in other ways, and it would be ungracious of you to prevent him (see *Presents*).

Other examples of well-directed kindness may be found in *Clothes (Men's)*, *What you Know*, *Meeting People*, *Getting On*, *Commemoration Balls*, *Dances*, *The Derby*, *The Flower Show*, *Escorts*, *Private Occasions*, *Conversation* (throughout), and indeed *passim* or everywhere, for this book might be described as a Guide to Kindness, and one small section cannot possibly contain all that the nice girl will make it her business to know about it.

TO WOMEN

Kindness to women falls into certain very definite classes. Most of these are referred to elsewhere: but to have them collected in one place and classified will, I hope, bring home to you how wide and varied are your opportunities for doing good.

Helping them to make the best of themselves. This includes helping them to find the right makeup (see *Pageants* and *Makeup*), pointing out what style of dressing suits them (see *Clothes, Other People's*), and unobtrusively helping them to remedy any little faults in their manners (see *Helping with a Party*).

But above all, the nice girl will want her friends to improve their characters. If you should hear people saying something unpleasant about any one of your friends, it is plainly your duty to tell her about it *at once*. It is probably a little exaggerated, but it may serve to draw her attention to some little personal fault of which she was quite unaware.

Seeing that they do not make friends with unsuitable people. If you know something really distressing about a friend of theirs, it is far kinder to tell them of it now than to leave them to find it out *afterward* or perhaps never find it out at all (see *Scandal*).

Giving them things. A generous girl will of course want to give her friends presents whenever she can (see *Presents*): but my concern at the moment is rather with the truer unselfishness of sharing your possessions with others. Trinkets, scarves, handbags, or even dresses which you *could* use again but are perfectly willing to sacrifice, can if given in the right spirit provoke real emotion in the friend to whom you are giving them. It is essential, of course, to offer them tactfully. Phrases such as the following would be perfectly apt.

"I'm sure this would fit you – it's *vast* on me."

"There's years of wear in it still."

"All my friends know it, but after all, yours won't."

"John won't let me wear it. He says it's too old for me."

"You think it's pretty? Well of course, if you *like* it, my dear, for heaven's sake take it."

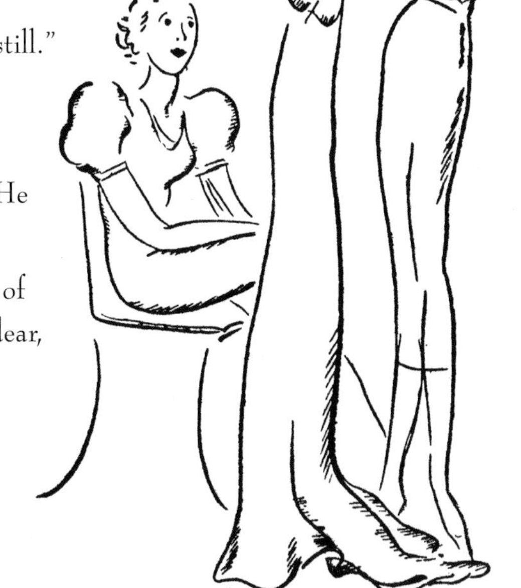

Praising them. Nothing is better proof of a sunny nature than to praise your friends *as much as you possibly can*. It will make them very happy (see also *Features*). There are all sorts of things that you could say, and I mention only a few.

"Darling, you've done your hair a new way. How *daring*!"

"What a charming hat. You look so *young* in it."

"I always like you in that old blue dress."

"You know, *really*, my dear, your complexion's quite good."

"I think you're so *brave* to wear spectacles."

"My dear, you're very *forgiving*."

And, if at some party, a man you both know seems to avoid complimenting your friend, it is thoughtful to draw his attention to the fact while you are both talking to her. Say, for example:

"Peter, you've never said a word about Joan's lovely dress – and it's new, too, isn't it, Joan?"

Or, "Isn't she looking *nice* tonight, darling?"

TO DEPENDENTS

It is a golden rule that nice people are nice even to those dependent on them, or to those who, through the injustice of fate, are in subordinate positions. True kindness, though, here as elsewhere, entails letting *no one* forget their place in the social system. After all, where would you be if *you* began getting above yourself? You might think you were the Queen. It is no less essential for maids, old governesses, shop assistants, and so forth to be frequently reminded of their place and encouraged to keep in it. The following points permit of no argument.

Maids are there to wait on you. Any help you require, at *any* time, it is their duty to give. You will allow no modernistic talk of their having other things to do, or of their wanting to get "off" for some so-called engagement. After all, as you will no doubt point out, you can surely be trusted to know what is good for them.

Shop assistants, again, have their job and are paid to do it. If after three-quarters of an hour or so they have shown you nothing but rubbish which you would not dream of buying, that is their fault. Give them, perhaps, another fifteen minutes to try and show you something tolerable; but at the end you will of course ignore all their shameless looks of reproach and walk coldly out of the shop without buying anything.

Charity is natural to a nature like yours. You give your services unreservedly to charity matinées, charity pageants, and charity bazaars, and do not think twice about the expense of the clothes such occasions oblige you to order. If you go to church, you will of course put *silver* into the collection. And if you were walking in the street with a friend, he would get some idea of your nature if you said, "Oh, look at that poor old woman, Walter. Haven't you a shilling to give her?"

TO OTHERS

In this class we may rank (1) your relations, and (2) any people whom you encounter casually.

1. For *relations*, you have little to do but follow the advice I have given in *Your Elders* (p. 83). It must be remembered, though, that you are less dependent on distant relations than on immediate ones; a second cousin once removed can do far less for you than, say, a generous grandmother. You will naturally want to be nicest to the people who do most for you. Common courtesy alone would demand it.

One thing must be remembered about relations. They are highly – indeed unnecessarily – sensitive. Things which you would do quite naturally to other people offend them so much that they prefer never to see you again; forgetting to thank them for a present, for example, or smiling at something they say. *This you cannot help*. That a boring relation is apt to take umbrage is no reason for not making an observation which anyone else would agree to be perfectly usual.

2. Among people whom you encounter casually may be ranked commissionaires, waitresses, taxi drivers, and servants in other people's houses. An *ordinary* person would feel almost obliged to give them a tip; but the nice, attractive young girl feels that a smile of thanks from her will bring far more pleasure than so sordid a gift as money.

3. Presents

RECEIVING

A. From Your Friends

That you will receive presents goes without saying. One of the few ways in which a man can show his affection for you is by giving you things, and you, we have already agreed, are not going to be so unkind as to refuse them (see p. 106). But there is an enormous variation in the grace with which girls receive presents. Some are so crude as to suggest that they will be even nicer to their friend, now he has given them a diamond-studded wristwatch, than they were before. As if gifts, however costly, could make *any* difference to the quality of one's affection! Others, again, will thank a man with equal coldness whether he gives them quite a good present, such as furs, or some nonsensical little mascot, which they can only pass on to the housemaid.

There is only one really gracious way to receive presents. Make it absolutely clear that no amount of generosity can affect the steadfast quality of your friendship; but, at the same time, *prove* that friendship by guiding his impulses into the most serviceable channels.

Supposing your friend longs to give you a dozen orchids; what could be more sensible than to say that orchids fade and you would rather have something more lasting (some trifle of jewelry, perhaps) to remember him by.

And if he says what can he do to show you how intense is his friendship for you, do not, as some girls would, smile and say pointlessly, "Nothing, darling." He has asked you because he wants to know. *Tell him*.

There is an outmoded idea that no girl should accept *wearing apparel* from a man she is fond of. It is thought by some people that to do so betokens an intimacy such as no nice girl should know any-

thing about at all. This of course is entirely mistaken. If a man wants to give you a dress or some underclothes, it means simply that his feelings for you are of a kind which can best be expressed in this manner. You will not, I know, be so behind the times as to put any difficulties in his way.

One word of warning, however. Supposing that a man, having loaded you (in spite of your protests) with gifts of every kind from jewels to evening underwear, begins to suggest that he expected you to feel – and even to *show* – rather warmer gratitude. Suppose he has the audacity to argue that, having *taken* certain things, you should be prepared to *give* certain things in exchange for them. What are you to think, and, still more urgent, what are you to say?

There is only one thing to think, and you must blame yourself deeply for not having realized it before. (See *How to Know Nice*

People, p. 33.) *This man is not a gentleman*. Tell him so, frankly. Point out that, had you known he had such a base mind, you would never have dreamed of accepting his presents, and absolutely refuse ever to receive any more. You will also make quite clear that you *prefer* never to set eyes on him again; but there are certain mitigations of this harsh sentence which often appeal to kind-hearted girls, and for these I advise you to turn to *Situations* (p. 127). Rigid though your standards of behavior must be, you do not, I know, want to miss any chance of helping your fellow-creatures.

B. From Others

You will also receive birthday and Christmas presents from your family and your intimate girl friends. It is sometimes difficult to receive these with suitable gratification. The best thing, in such a case, is to go on saying, "*Oh. Oh. Oh, Laura*" (or "*Oh, Auntie*") until they are forced to put in "Well, you like it, then?", thus as it were taking the words out of your mouth. But there are few girls so ungrateful that they cannot realise they are after all receiving a *present*, and manage some little conventional exclamation such as "How exquisite!" "How adorable!" or "Why, that's just what I wanted!"

It is nice to show that you really appreciate a present. After you have thanked the giver, you should add, if you can "But how terribly kind of you – this must have cost at *least* half a crown." I need hardly say that you will put this estimate on the *low* side. You would cause great embarrassment were you to name a higher sum than she has actually paid.

GIVING

A. To Men

It is a universal rule that no nice girl gives presents to a man. This may make you unhappy, but, like all other rules, it is based on consideration for him. You give a man many things; your friendship, your understanding, your sympathy, your companionship. You *take* from him presents (see p. 112), because it is your duty to allow him to make what return he can. He would be unhappy if you did not let him. Consider how he would feel if, in addition to all that you do for him, you started giving him presents. He would be *wretched*, realising that you were doing something for which he could make no return. To cause unhappiness is the *very last* thing you want to do.

B. To Others

You will naturally want to give presents on suitable occasions to your parents, your brothers and sisters, your very dear schoolfriends, some of your aunts, and so forth. But you must always remember that there is a danger of embarrassing people if you continually load them with sumptuous and expensive presents, and that it is the *thought* rather than the expenditure which counts. If as a general rule you try to give only *inexpensive* presents, you will avoid this danger entirely.

I need hardly point out that you must be *especially* careful to give presents to people who are always generous to you. Grandmothers, rich aunts, godfathers, and so forth often expend large sums of money upon a really nice young girl. It is true they do not *miss* the money in the least; but nevertheless, you want to show that you are grateful, and some tiny token each year will prove to them that, if they do not forget *your* birthday, you do not forget *theirs*.

4. LOVE

TRUE

Love, it is well known, is the most beautiful and the strongest of all the emotions, and the one that has the most wonderful consequences. So much has been written about it, since the beginning of the world, by poets, novelists, doctors, etc., that young girls often feel the *greatest* ambition to experience this magic sensation. More unhappiness is caused by their eagerness than by almost anything else; for they tend to mistake for love things *that are not love at all*, and to throw themselves body and soul, so to speak, into courses of action that are bound to prove a snare and a delusion.

Fortunately for us all, there is one absolutely *infallible* way of telling true love from its imitations. It is *essential* for the nice girl to take my next words to heart, for by them she will stand or fall. If she ignores them, all her kindness, all her thoughtfulness and unselfishness may come to nothing, and she might just as well not have read this book at all.

True love leads to marriage. If a man falls in love with you, he will ask you to become publicly engaged to him, and thus, in course of time, you will marry. That is all. That is the infallible test by which love may be recognized, and there is absolutely no other. I do not say, you will notice, that one kind of love leads to marriage, and another to *this*, and another to *that*, and so forth. I say that love leads to one course, and one alone. The nice girl will not forget it.

So if ever you tend, as girls do, to grow romantic and imagine you have fallen in love, you must search your mind very carefully and

apply this test to find out whether you have done so or not. Is the object of your so-called affections unmarried? If divorced, is he *completely* so? Is he able to support a wife in proper comfort? Has he a mother who might want to live with him? Would he be away all day, and not moping about at home? And finally, does he, by unmistakable references to partnership, settling down, home life, and meeting his mother make it perfectly clear that he is the kind of man to whom a nice girl can entrust her affections?

If you can answer all these questions suitably, then you are in love. And if you cannot, *you are not*.

(For further information see Part V.)

There are, however, certain less overwhelming emotions which you may quite well feel while waiting for true love to come to you. These milder emotions may be broadly divided into two classes, which are best distinguished as *Friendship* and *Affection*.

FRIENDSHIP

Friendship with a man can often be a thing of great beauty. It is as it were a *private* relationship. It concerns you and him only, and as long as your circle of friends know nothing about it they will think nothing about it at all. You alone know how much you mean to the man. Let me again emphasize that there is no question of love. He may even be married, or determined for some quaint reason never to become so. Provided he is nice (see p. 33), such accidents of fate do not move you. It is for what he *is* that you have become his friend.

And also, of course, it is for what he *needs*. He needs you. He needs your conversation, your advice, your encouragement, your criticism, your presence, your trust, your kindness. In fact, to put it in a nutshell, he needs your friendship. You would be by no means the person I take you for if you were to refuse it.

AFFECTION

Affection may be defined as what you feel for a man for whom you cannot feel friendship. You may feel affection for all sorts of people; for politicians, for retired colonels, and even for your uncles or your father's bachelor friends. It is a delightful manifestation. Unlike friendship, which, as I said, is a *private* concern, it flourishes best in public. It can there afford some very moving sights. For example:

It can lead nice young girls to go to the Chelsea Flower Show with men old enough to be their grandfathers (see p. 53).

It can impel a girl to stand for three hours or more in a marsh, with an east wind blowing and in steady rain, to observe the habits of the lesser spotted sandpiper with a wealthy old landowner.

Instances could be multiplied; but there are few things more beautiful than affection in perfect flower, and the girl who is unselfish enough to allow herself to feel it will find that her old friend's pleasure and gratitude are a quite unlooked-for reward.

MINOR COMPLICATIONS

From the poets, etc., to whom I have referred, and even from some of your girl friends, you might gather that there are certain kinds of love which, though undeniably *true*, are not altogether *happy*. For example:

Unrequited love.
Unsuitable love.
Despised love.
Concealed love.
Frantic love.
Hopeless love.

These, you will be told, happen as often to girls as they do to men. *This is wrong*. You have only to remember my definition of true love to realise what a gross error your informants are making.

You do not suffer unrequited love, despised love, hopeless love, etc. Some underbred girls may have the appalling lack of dignity to imagine themselves in such a position – loving a man who does not love them, loving someone unsuitable, and so forth. *You know what love is*. You know that unless it is mutual, and suitable, and with marriage as its only conceivable aim, *it is not love at all*. You will act accordingly.

It may happen at times, though, that you experience sensations which are quite new to you and which you might if unwarned have suspected of being love. You may, for instance, think that So-and-so (a very ordinary man) is the most beautiful person you have ever set eyes on. Your heart may beat so hard when he comes into the room that it almost chokes you. And yet So-and-so is (shall we say) a preparatory schoolmaster, with very little money apart from his pay and with very little interest apart from small boys. *This is not love*. Or Edward Blank, apparently devoted to you, has gone away to South America without remembering to say good-bye. You lose your appetite. You are unable to sleep, to eat, to do anything except revisit all the places which you and he used to visit together, and there shed tears. Some girls would go about bragging – literally bragging – of an unhappy love affair. You, being sensible, know that your condition is due only to unseasonable weather.

I do not say that girls may not, on meeting a very nice man, feel some little warning inside them which says "Here is a man I could love." Womanly intuition is a precious possession, and I am the last person to want to cry it down. If this should ever happen to you, and if careful inquiries should reveal that the man is indeed one who could rouse true love in you, you are then in a very happy position. You will *be a friend to him*. You will make it your business to be with him as much as possible, and foster that kinship which is bound to arise between minds so perfectly attuned to each other. If at any time friendship should ripen into love, you will realize that he, with a boldness of concept which would never have occurred to you has looked into the future and seen that understanding such as exists between you now would make the perfect basis for a happy marriage. Surprised though you will be when he reveals his thoughts, *you should believe him*.

But to turn back to the darker aspects of the picture. Those conditions which the poets speak of (despised, hopeless, unrequited, etc., love) do in point of fact exist. For you, happily they do not; but it cannot be denied that for *men* they do. And, knowing this – knowing that men are unhappy – you will I am sure have only one impulse. You will want to be kind to them.

Here, as elsewhere, your opportunities are unlimited. They fall, broadly speaking, into two classes. (1) Sometimes, through no fault whatever of your own, a man may be unhappy because of *you*. (2) Sometimes he may be unhappy because of *some other girl*. The circumstances are different, but the remedy in each case is much the same.

(1) If a man loves you and you cannot return his love, there is no one to blame but Fate. You would *like* to love him; but Fate has so arranged it that one of the essential factors is lacking (see p. 116), and without this, as you well know, *love is not possible*. But this fact,

unfortunately, weighs very little with a man who is really infatuated. He will believe that things can all be put right somehow – that poverty can become riches, and heaven knows what besides. He will hope to over-persuade you; and no matter how much you try to discourage him, he is certain to want to go on seeing you whenever he possibly can. Well, *you must let him*. You must *be kind* to him. Have him invited to your home a lot. Go out whenever he asks you, and even be a little bold and suggest a few outings yourself. It may, in a way, be torture to him to be with you; but you can be very certain it would be a far worse torture to be kept away.

(2) If a friend of yours has been cruelly treated by another girl, *now is your chance*. I mean of course now is your chance to be really, lastingly helpful. Be kind to this man, even if he fancies he is still in love with the tasteless and uneducated girl in question. See a lot of him. Have him, too, asked to your home a lot (see above), and suggest little outings which will make him forget his troubles and take him out of himself. Be a friend to him (see *Friendship*). Show him that there are some girls who can be trusted, who have a serious outlook on life, who appreciate quality and personality in a man when they see it. It is only a question of time before you win him to a saner, happier view of existence. When you do, he will be the first to admit that it is to you he owes it all, and he will long that you should share in his newfound contentment.

The Nice Girl's Guide

PART IV

ADVANCED INSTRUCTION

The more you go about the world and meet people, and the more you try to live up to your principle of kindness to everyone, the more you will discover that life is not as simple as it ought to be. Complications are apt to arise with astounding rapidity.

The nice girl faces this calmly. Her conscience clear, her good intentions undaunted, she lets nothing perturb her, but continues to try and learn yet *more* ways of helping people, even if they are not wholly to her advantage. The following pages chart the main problems she is likely to have to face.

I. SYMPATHY

Sympathy, one of the best and most unselfish emotions, is one which is all too often misunderstood. You will find as you grow a little older that you cannot avoid it even if you wanted to; people who are lonely or unhappy will claim more and more of your attention, but you will also find, the world being what it is, that your actions are apt to be grossly misinterpreted.

This, I admit, can be inconvenient, and if your conscience were not so perfectly clear it might at times make you unhappy. But no nice girl ever allowed inconvenience to deter her from doing her duty, and I give the following survey of the field for sympathy in the full conviction that it will be put to practical use.

The lonely – Men whose wives or fiancées have thoughtlessly gone away on visits, or, worse still, have left them altogether.

The sensitive – This includes a pathetically large number of people, for far more men are sensitive than their immediate relations ever find out. A girl who is sensitive herself realises such things very quickly. Among men of this kind one would obviously class young poets, unsuccessful painters, and all in fact who have felt the call of Art. With such people it is sometimes necessary to use *culture* (see *Culture*), but the really sympathetic woman will find other ways of winning them back to happiness.

The unsatisfied – There are many men who have not found their proper niche in life; square pegs in round holes, so to speak, who are doing things that they do not care about and perhaps do not know what it is that they *want* to do. Feminine sympathy, suggesting fresh

avenues of interest and urging a fuller, broader life, may make all the difference to people like this.

The browbeaten or henpecked – It is in some ways a sign of niceness if a man allows himself to be browbeaten by a mother, elder sister, or wife. It shows that he is chivalrous to women; but the pathetic, lost look in such a man's eyes is a mute appeal that few nice girls could resist. To allow such a man to *realize* himself; to take him away from his unhappy surroundings and teach him that he *has* power, that he *has* the capacity for enjoyment, is the very truest sort of kindness.

The misunderstood – This is by far the largest class of unhappy people. It is *astonishing* to see how many men are misunderstood by their wives or others. It gives the nice girl a terrible insight into the blindness of her sex in general, and the crying need for a more widespread dissemination of kindness.

The moment a man begins to tell a girl that his wife does not understand him, she will realize that he is making a tacit appeal for her sympathy. A few gentle questions, some warm expressions of censure, and a courteously phrased wish that life might be happier for him, will clearly prove to him that he has at last found somebody who *does* understand him.

2. SITUATIONS

Situations, as I have said, are all too often the unjust result of giving rein to one's natural sympathy. They arise purely from misunderstanding or unworthy distrust, and the nice girl, finding herself suddenly involved in one, will *instantly* seek for the kindest way of putting everybody at their ease and making them happy again. The following pages, I think, should amply prepare her for any momentary awkwardness she is likely to meet.

The nice girl, her friend, and another man

If another man arrives in the room at a moment when she and her friend are in *serious* conversation, the nice girl, after a rapid mental decision, will make the most suitable of the following remarks:

"Oh, Mr. Robinson, you have mistaken your way."

"Clear out, Bertie."

"I am trying to get some dust out of poor Freddie's eye."

"I look upon Fred as a brother."

"Don't be such a fool."

The nice girl, her friend, and a parent

Here again I have provided for several emergencies, and it is best to study the facts before selecting the most appropriate reply.

"Father! Save me!"

"Oh, Daddy, this is Mr. Wilkinson."

"Lend me a handkerchief, will you? Fred has something in his eye."

"Mummy, darling – how nice that you've come. Fred is just going to ask me to marry him."

The nice girl, her friend, and her friend's wife

It is possible that the wife, on her tactless intrusion, will have made certain remarks before the nice girl has a chance to explain the purity of her motives. If not, however, the following observations are appropriate.

"Hullo, darling, you're late. We were getting quite anxious about you."

"Selina, I pity you."

"Your husband tells me that he has a fly in his eye."

"Edward is just like a father to me."

"You have a vulgar mind."

"My dear, I'm only trying to make up to Edward a little for all he has missed."

The nice girl, her friend, and a maidservant

"Mr. Lomax and I are discussing business. Go away."

It is often thoughtful to remind an intrusive maidservant that even in the midst of your private worries you do not forget her welfare. In such a case you should say:

"By the way, Mary, I was meaning to give you that pale-blue dress you admired so much. You may go and take it *now*, if you like to."

It is almost certain that the maid in her pleasure will quite forget she has seen you and Mr. Lomax together.

The nice girl, her friend, and a girl of less sensitive nature

Realizing how few other girls live up to her own high ideals, the nice girl will be prepared to find them a little *suspicious* should they intrude when she is quietly talking with one of her friends. Any of the following remarks should put matters right.

"Never mind, Patty – I dare say you'll have someone to talk to yourself, one day."

"Run away, darling."

"I'm busy."

"Poor Walter had a fly in his eye."

"Oh, Pamela – I've just been telling Walter *all* about you and poor Georgie Horrocks."

Most situations, as you will have gathered, contain three people. There is one situation, however (unhappily all too common), which concerns two people only. It may be described as:

The nice girl and a man whom she did not understand

It sometimes happens that, just because a nice girl shows him sympathy, a man imagines he can ask her *almost anything* (see *Presents*, p. 112). Some men, after only a dinner, a theater, and perhaps a night club, imagine they can demand sympathy of a kind to which even the closest of personal friends are hardly entitled. Her responses to such a man are a matter of absolute certainty. She will make any or all of the following:

"I assure you, Mr. Hartlepool, you have made a mistake."

"We were so happy, and now you've spoiled it all."

"Don't do that."

"Who do you imagine I am?" or

"What do you take me for?"

"But we hardly know each other."

"I wish I had never taken your presents, if that's what you think of me." (It would however be discourteous to offer to give them all back.)

"Let's talk about something different."

"You seem to imagine I'm a gold digger."

"I am horrified."

If, however, the man's nature seems to be capable of improvement, a really understanding girl would hold out hopes that this lapse might be overlooked. She would hint that he might in time qualify for her affection or even her friendship (see p. 118), and would suggest further meetings in order that they might find out whether this were probable.

3. Unpleasantness

I distinguish *Unpleasantness* from *Situations* because, unlike most of these, it occurs between two people only, and, unfortunately, between people who have been on terms of *real friendship*. The following notes will give some idea of its many manifestations.

Sometimes, when a girl who has done a *great deal* for a man endeavors to improve his character in some tiny way, he will become quite unduly enraged and swear vehemently that he never wants to see her again.

Sometimes, for no reason whatsoever, a man will announce to a girlfriend that he has a new girlfriend whom he *prefers* to her.

Sometimes, on seeing her in public with some other friend, a man will without further inquiry assume that his girlfriend has become tired of him, and will reproach her with *all sorts* of things.

Sometimes men are rude about a girl's character.

Sometimes men are discourteous to girls about their appearance.

Sometimes a man whom a girl has actually *seen about* with some other girl will protest that he meant nothing by it and that even if he did she has no business to mind.

Sometimes men believe rumors about a girlfriend which are spread by *malicious* and *ill-natured* people (see *Scandal*).

This bleak statement of facts gives no account of the anguish that can be caused by *Unpleasantness*, but the girl of sensitive nature will be able to imagine it for herself. She will not, however, let it affect her behavior. Refined and dignified as always, she will in the face of whatever provocation make *no* remark that is not calm and reasonable. The following would suit their respective occasions perfectly.

"I wish her joy of you, I'm sure."

"You cur."*

"You cad."*

"You coward."*

"I'll tell Mummie."

"Go, then. You are not worthy of me."

"Well, Maisie is a liar."*

"I despise you from the bottom of my heart."

"*So you say.*"

"If you think I mind, you're mistaken."*

"I *won't* be quiet."

Many girls will feel that occasions such as we are dealing with permit, and even *demand*, a certain vigour of language (see *Language*). Fully perceiving their point of view, I have marked with an asterisk the phrases on the above list where a forceful epithet could be suitably introduced.

Unpleasantness of these kinds hardly ever takes place without a certain amount of insult. Once more I must remind you not to let this make you unhappy (see p. 105). Your conscience is clear. Your late friend may mean all he says, for the moment, for he is in a state where he cannot distinguish truth from falsehood. But no one would believe him (except lovers of *Scandal*, for which see p. 136). No one of a pure and impartial mind would believe for an instant that you are, shall we say, a certain debased type of woman to which in his frenzy he has compared you. Knowing this, your mind is at rest.

4. SCANDAL

A. Concerning Yourself

The world is a very ill-natured place, and the nicer and kinder a girl tries to be, the more jealous and unsuccessful people will spread heartless rumors about her. It would be pleasant to be able to ignore such rumors; but you will find that all your friends show the utmost eagerness to tell you about them, owing to their envy of your superior character.

There are only two ways of silencing scandal. One is *admission*, the other *explanation*. *Denial*, which seems the obvious way, is of no use at all, as people judge you by themselves and promptly suspect you of lying. Admission and explanation often overlap, as the following examples will show.

"No, Henry and I are no longer engaged. Mummie decided that he was a little too old for me."

"Oh, yes, I was at the White Hart last Tuesday. I *do* wish I'd seen you, darling. Adolph's old mother was a little upset by the heat, and we were waiting for her to come out of the Ladies' Cloak-room."

"I *allow* Philip to take other girls out to dinner. I *like* him to do it."

"Yes, of course, I'm *devoted* to Richard." (This is a brilliant reply, as it admits an obvious fact while making quite clear that you do not feel the kind of affection for Richard which they all imagine you feel.)

"Yes, I often go out with Michael. He misses his wife so *terribly*."

If it should happen that you are *not* told what people are saying about you, but guess from their manner that scandalous tongues are at work, the best thing to do is use your intuition. Say to yourself, "If I were *not* of a nice nature, and perceived another girl doing certain deeds of kindness like those I am doing for So-and-so, *what might I think*?" Ten to one you will be able to puzzle out the answer.

B. Scandal Concerning Other People

I need hardly say that you will pay not the slightest heed to ill-natured gossip either about your friends or about people unknown to you. Indeed, where it concerns your friends you will take every possible opportunity to contradict it. You may often know something which would rule the scandalmonger's insinuations right out of court, and in this case it will be your duty as well as your pleasure to make your knowledge public. The following remarks occur to me:

"Well, it can't have been William. He's very busy, I happen to know, in *quite* another direction."

"Mary, my dear? No, no, you've made a mistake. Poor girl, she only wishes that that sort of thing did happen to her."

"Jane and Archibald? What a wicked thing to say. Why, Archibald's *married*."

"Philip's *not* a sponger. I know Mrs. Lovell gives him all his suits, but she *told* me, she looks on him almost as a son."

"John with a *girl*, my dear? Rubbish. I can tell you for a fact, *he isn't that sort*."

Your careful avoidance of scandalmongering must not, however, be allowed to blunt your innate critical faculties. Scandal is one thing. An intelligent interest in other people's characters is another. It comes naturally to a perceptive mind, and you owe it to yourself and your friends not to stifle this precious quality.

Thus, if you *know* that one of your friends says things which he does not mean, or is miserly, or loses his temper over tennis or bridge, there is no point in pretending that you think him the most honest, the most generous, the most sportsmanlike man you have ever met. Indeed, such deception would be *wrong*; by withholding such information you might cause another of your friends to make some irreparable blunder.

In this as in all things, your conduct can only be guided by the

abstract principles of kindness. What is the *kind* thing to do? Is it to let all your friends accept Horace as perfect, and then find out, *perhaps too late*, what you could have told them all along? Or is it to give them some gentle warning – the merest hint – of his peculiar disabilities, and leave them to decide for themselves what intimacy is possible? Your conscience will give you the answer better than I can.

Or supposing you know things about the red-headed girl whom Charlie So-and-so admires which will almost break his heart when he gets to know of them. Are you going to leave him to become more and more enamored of her, only to find out, *too late*, that she is not worthy of his devotion? Are you going to keep silent, where silence might have such *overwhelming* results? I will not insult you by supplying your answer.

THE NICE GIRL'S GUIDE

PART V
CAUSE AND EFFECT

Almost without exception, nice girls get married. It has already been proved (see p. 116) that true love leads to marriage, and few girls are so warped and insensitive that they do not at some time or another find it natural to fall in love. People of low nature have been known to say that young girls *try* to get married; that efforts at kindness and sympathy, such as those set down in this book, are in point of fact all inspired by the hope of finding a husband.

They do not realize that the whole thing is a question of cause and effect. If a girl is nice, she will win a good man's love and will thus get married. That is all. You do your best, you try to be kind and helpful, simply because you have high ideals. If it happens at some time that a nice man asks you to marry him, you will, I know, be taken quite by surprise.

You will welcome his suggestion as giving you many new opportunities of doing good to others.

I. ENGAGEMENTS

A. Your Own

It is often difficult to make the perfect reply to congratulations upon your engagement, owing to the state of ecstatic confusion in which you are apt to find yourself. The following, I hope, may help you.

"Thank you, Angela darling. I only wish we could manage to find someone for you."

"I shan't be rich like you, dear – but they *will* know I'm not marrying Hubert for his money."

"I know that marriage isn't everything – but then, I haven't your brains!"

"I wish I wasn't marrying quite so young, though. I'd love to have knocked about for years, like you."

"Thanks so much, darling. It's funny, isn't it, that you knew Peter all those years! You must go on seeing him, often."

"I believe John *will* come into some money some day. I knew I could trust you to tell me all about that."

B. Other People's

News of your friends' engagements is bound to give you great pleasure, and you will be anxious to prove this to them by some enthusiastic remark. The following are both individual and generous.

"Darling, how *exciting*. Which of them is it?"

"My dear, it's superb. People simply wouldn't believe me."

"Why, you're looking years younger already!"

"After all, my dear, what does poverty matter?"

"I always maintained that you'd marry."

2. WEDDINGS

A. Your Own

The question of weddings hardly comes within the scope of my survey; but the following isolated notes will give you certain opportunities of living up to your own ideals which I should not like you to miss.

Remember that you can gauge people's friendship for you by the wedding presents they give. Now, of all times, people will want to prove the real depth of their affection for you; and you will readily understand that the friend who gives plated teaspoons does not hold you as dear as the friend who offers a large canteen full of solid silver.

This is an invaluable guide for the future, and the thoughtful girl will send out as many wedding invitations as possible, in order that the largest available number of friends may be able to testify to the warmth of their friendship.

It is only fair to your future husband to make yourself look as nice as you possibly can on your wedding day. For once you must consider *yourself* a little. Remember that the bridal retinue is to do you honor, not to give the bridesmaids a chance to exhibit themselves. If they should complain that pink does not suit them, or that orange makes them look sallow, you must I am afraid resist all impulses to give in to them.

If they continue their protests, you might remonstrate pleasantly, "Well, Doreen darling, why not get married yourself?"

Everyone loves the privilege of helping at a wedding, so do not deny people this, or feel that in allowing them to pack for you, sew for you, write letters, run errands, dress you, and so forth, you are giving them the very slightest trouble. They will probably remember this wonderful occasion till their dying day.

B. Other People's

If you are a guest at some friend's wedding, you will be as loyal to her then as you are at all other times. It is a polite convention that the most beautiful, most radiant, and most noteworthy person at any wedding is always agreed to be the bride. You will do your *utmost* to fall in with this tradition. Try to discover something about her that you can honestly praise. For example:

> "How happy she looks – and she ought to. She's worked hard enough for it."
>
> "That veil right over her face is very becoming."
>
> "This subdued light is perfect."
>
> "What self-control! *I* couldn't look so placid, if I were marrying him."

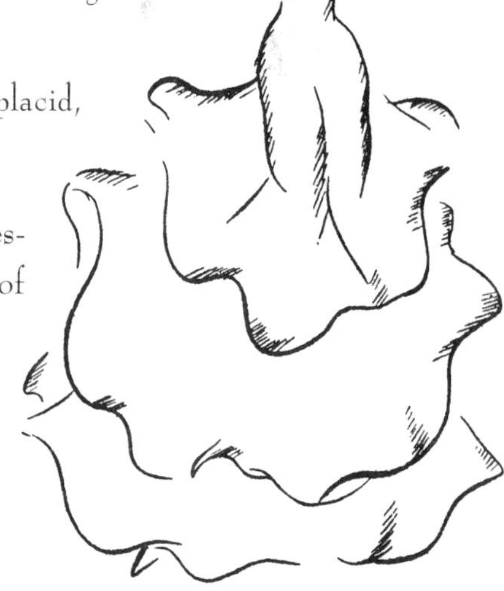

If you *can* praise the bridegroom, the bridesmaids, the church decorations, etc., you will of course be anxious to do so. If you find that you cannot, it is best to remark "My dear, don't let's say a *word* about the bridesmaids," and your friends will perfectly understand your chivalrous wish to keep silence.

It is customary not to talk above a murmur while the church ceremony is in progress.

Should one of your friends ask you to act as her bridesmaid, remember that she means this as a compliment. She will imagine that the honour of attending her far outweighs all the trouble and expense to which you will be put.

You should accept, because it will make her happy; but do not let her imagine that she can therefore ask you to do all sorts of menial tasks for her, such as unpacking presents, arranging flowers, and even writing her letters. There are other people simply *longing* to do all this sort of thing; your duty is to keep as fresh as you can, to do her credit on the actual day of the wedding.

However much you dislike showing yourself off, remember that a wedding is a *Public Occasion* in that it enables you to meet people who might be glad of your friendship. Best men, ushers, etc., can often be wonderfully helped in the discharge of their duties by a little sympathy on the part of one of the bridesmaids.

3. Other Contingencies

It is more than unlikely that there will be any other development of your potentialities but that provided by love and marriage. You ought however to know that there *can* be other developments. A knowledge of the sadder side of life does nothing but good to the person of real sensibility, and, though I feel confident that none of the following occupations will ever appeal to you, you will nevertheless be all the better for knowing that they exist.

A. Looking After One's Parents

Some girls, after several years of ordinary pursuits during which they have somehow failed to find any man who loves them, realize that their true mission in life is to stay at home and look after their aging parents. For such unselfishness you can have nothing but admiration.

B. Going for a Cruise

Even quite young girls sometimes feel that if they were to go on a cruise they might have special opportunities of meeting lonely and unhappy people who wanted companionship. It is a general rule that the older people get the more this conviction increases.

C. Going Abroad

Those who have gone out to India, Malta, or even Egypt say that the pleasure that can be given to lonely Empire builders by the visit of a white woman completely repays any trifling inconvenience that may be experienced in making the journey. It is notable that a large percentage of the girls who go out there find the opportunities of doing good so extensive that they do not come back.

D. Marrying Quietly

There are occasions when even girls of quite irreproachable nature find a quiet wedding more to their taste than an ordinary one. When you hear of this happening, you must try to put yourself in the place of your friend and find out why she is doing it. To *understand*, you will find, will be to *excuse*. She may, shall we say, have a rooted objection to being gazed at by inquisitive crowds.

It sometimes happens that a girl who is genuinely in love (see p. 116) has to wait for her friend to be divorced by his wife before he is free to marry her. Gossip is apt, however unfairly, to mention her name in connection with the divorce proceedings, and as the co-respondent's name will be kept out of court, she has no way of proving her innocence. She will be careful, however, to make clear by the decorum of her behavior in all public places that such rumors are base and unwarranted.

And remember that *marriage is marriage*, and once a girl has become married people will quite forget after a year or two whether she was married quietly or in the ordinary way.

E. Social Work

It is by no means rare for even quite young girls to take an interest in Girl Guides, Infant Welfare, and other invaluable social avocations. Gradually, however, as their interests broaden, they perceive that they have really better ways of doing good elsewhere, and it is only those whose heart is *exclusively* in such work who go on doing it, year in, year out, with such wonderful and indefatigable zest. To them, you will say, all praise.

F. Living Alone

Women in these days have to face many problems, and it sometimes happens that young girls feel they cannot be fully themselves unless they are free to go off and live somewhere alone. This happens especially to girls whose parents do not live in London. As long as they have a friend to visit them, and a little *pied à terre* where no one comes uninvited, they feel they will be able to face life more completely, and have peace and quiet to think things out for themselves. And who can say that they may not be perfectly right? As I said before, to *understand* is to *excuse*.

Sometimes these girls go out to work all day, preferring to have some occupation for the long hours when they must be alone. Others stay in, engrossed all the time with their little hobbies and their thoughts; and if occasionally, in the evenings, they hear the latchkey of the friend who is coming to ask for their consolation and advice, they feel that all their sacrifices are well rewarded.

ENVOI

All nice girls have marked individuality, and I do not for a moment suppose that all the advice in the foregoing survey will be of equal use to them all. Different personalities cause different things to happen, and where one girl may go on being nice without rousing comment from anybody, another, with precisely similar aims and ideals, may find that scandal, situations, etc., spring up wherever she goes.

But this book allows for all variations of character. Its one requirement is niceness and kindness of heart. The remarks which it offers you have all been tried out by people of widely assorted temperaments, and where one does not suit your particular taste the next, I hope, will do so.

A thorough acquaintance with all possibilities should broaden your outlook and enable you at all times to *say* and to *do* the thing that will cause the most widespread pleasure to everyone.

If this little handbook teaches even a few idealistic young girls to voice their natural sentiments, I shall feel it has amply succeeded.

INDEX